ART STYLES OF THE PAPUAN GULF

Details: 1 Pendant figure (mimia). Lower Fly
River area. See fig. 62. 2 Agiba. Kerewa area.
Cambridge 1916.14383. 3 Bull-roarer. Purari
Delta: Namau. See fig. 40a. 4 Ancestral board
(hohao). Vailala: Elema. Chicago 142128

ART STYLES OF THE PAPUAN GULF

by Douglas Newton

The Museum of Primitive Art, New York. Distributed by University Publishers, Inc.,
New York
1961

Contents

Copyright 1961, The Museum of Primitive Art,
15 West 54 Street, New York 19, New York

Printed in the United States of America
by Connecticut Printers, Inc., Hartford

Design by Douglas Newton

ACKNOWLEDGMENT

Lenders to the exhibition

Mr. Serge Brignoni, Mr. Eliot Elisofon, Mr. Allan Frumkin, Mr. and Mrs. Aaron Furman, Mr. Heker Jensen, Mr. and Mme Henri Kamer, Mr. Herbert F. Rieser, Mr. and Mrs. Robert J. Sainsbury, Mr. and Mrs. Gustave Schindler, Mr. and Mrs. Raymond Wielgus, Dr. and Mrs. Ernest B. Zeisler; and two collectors who wish to remain anonymous. Koninklijk Instituut voor de Tropen, Amsterdam; The Brooklyn Museum; Buffalo Museum of Science; Chicago Natural History Museum; Dartmouth College Museum; National Museum of Ireland, Dublin; Peabody Museum of Archaeology and Ethnology, Harvard; The University Museum, Philadelphia.

Sources of illustrations

Ralph Altman no. 124
The Art Institute of Chicago no. 72
The Baltimore Museum of Art no. 64
The British Museum nos. 66, 92, 111, 119, 222, 225
Chicago Natural History Museum nos. 4, 40e, 42, 69, 71, 75, 76, 90, 91, 107, 120, 236
Robert David no. 48b
Dr. Douglas Fraser nos. 9, 61, 86, 198, 247, 249, 255, 260
Allan Frumkin no. 110
H. Gowers no. 226
Whitney Halstead nos. 67, 68, 70, 88, 89, 134
Capt. Frank Hurley nos. 20, 40b, 40c, 48a, 182, 183, 184, 185, 186, 190, 191, 192, 208
A. B. Lewis (courtesy Chicago Natural History Museum) nos. 28, 31, 32, 33, 34, 35, 39, 43, 109, 218, 219, 220, 238, 239, 241
Elisabeth G. Little no. 257

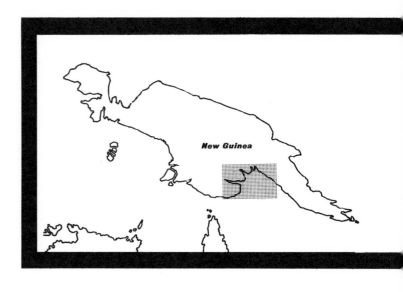

INTRODUCTION

The remarkable qualities of Papuan Gulf art have long been recognized: almost from the first incursions of missionaries and government officials into the area, examples found their way into the museums of Europe. For some seventy years the area has also been the chosen field of many distinguished anthropologists: Haddon, Landtman, Williams and Wirz being among the most prominent. All of them collected; most were highly conscious of the role of art in the societies. The objects themselves were the subject of important early studies in primitive art, and were described and analyzed in Haddon's pioneering work *The Decorative Art of British New Guinea*, published in 1894. At that time, however, the material available from the eastern and central areas of the Gulf was still sparse, and the western area virtually unknown. No general account of the art styles has appeared since. It seemed worthwhile, therefore, to illustrate in this book—prepared in conjunction with an exhibition at the Museum of Primitive Art— a representative group of objects from the whole area.

The gratitude of the Museum of Primitive Art is due to the many institutions and individuals who generously helped in the preparation of the exhibition by lending objects from their collections. Many others also contributed greatly to the book by unstinting permission to reproduce their photographs. Special thanks are due to Mr. Cory Reynolds of the Museum's staff for his research and editorial assistance. Finally I am grateful to Mr. K. J. Hewett, in whose collection I first saw examples of Papuan Gulf art.

Douglas Newton

1 THE PAPUAN GULF COUNTRY AND THE PEOPLE

6 *Map of the Papuan Gulf area. See also map facing p. 100.*
7 *"Life in New Guinea in 1877": a missionary view. From James Chalmers, Work and Adventure in New Guinea*

The central part of New Guinea's southern coast line describes an enormous bay, some two hundred miles across, known as the Papuan Gulf. Its shore, and the banks of the rivers which flow into it, are the home of numerous tribes whose creative genius has made this one of the most fertile art-producing areas of the island.

The existence of the great waterway between New Guinea and Australia was established by the voyage of the Portuguese navigator Luis Vaez de Torres in 1606; Bampton and Alt of the East India Company sighted the Gulf coasts in 1793, and Captain Blackwood of HMS "Fly" visited them in 1845. A first rough survey was made by Captain Owen Stanley in 1849 during the HMS "Rattlesnake" expedition. Apart from these minor incidents, the colonial policy of the Dutch during the 18th century, and British concentration on the settlement of Australia during the 19th, diverted attention from the area for over two hundred and fifty years. However, a growing consciousness throughout the 1870's on the part of the Australians of the strategic implications of New Guinea's geographical situation, coupled with the discovery of gold deposits, led to Queensland's annexing the whole eastern half of the island in 1883. A British protectorate over the southeast sector alone was formally proclaimed in the following year. Eventually it was taken under the control of the Commonwealth of Australia in 1906, with the name of the Territory of Papua.

In the particular area treated in this book—that part of the Gulf coast which extends from Cape Possession in the east to the Fly River in the west—the cultures fall into several groups. To the east are the Elema tribes, a coastal people. In the center are the Namau tribes of the Purari Delta, and those inhabiting the rivers just west of it, and the islands at their mouths. West of these again is a group of distinct but allied cultures, the richest being that of the Kerewa-speaking people of the river estuaries and their islands. The most westerly cultures of all to be mentioned here are the Kiwai in the Fly River estuary, and the Gogodara well inland and to the north of them.

In the early days of contact, the tribes had an evil reputation for hostility and dubious morals, and for an intense conservatism in their adherence to these ways. Many of their customs, erotic and murderous, seemed to verge upon insanity; only the later researches of anthropologists disclosed their purposes and logic. Today none of these societies exists in its pristine form, of course; the descriptions given here are written and must be read as merely in the historic present. Even so, in spite of missionary activity and the desire of the people themselves for the advantages of western civilization, much of their traditional way of life has shown a remarkable durability. The ceremonial houses of the Namau tribes subsisted until 1950; the latest performance of a great ritual cycle (Semese) by the eastern Elema took place about the same date.

The people of the Gulf area are Papuans distinct in language, culture and physique from the Melanesians who inhabit the eastward coast and its archipelagoes. How or when they came to settle around the Gulf is unknown; it has been suggested that their ancestors arrived on the northeast coast of the island and moved up the Sepik River valley, crossed the central mountain ranges, and—still following the courses of great rivers—fanned out southwards to the Gulf and southwest into what is now Netherlands New Guinea. Trade still exists along these routes. Such a theory helps to account for the many traits held in common by the Iatmul of the Sepik River; the people of the Gulf itself; the Marind-anim and the Asmat of southwest New Guinea; and the lesser groups neighboring these powerful groups.

It may be said of all these societies, that they are stubbornly democratic through aggressive individualism, only acknowledging the existence of "big men"—the heads of clans—with wealth and influence. Practice varies, but these headmen are usually regarded without particular deference. The tribesmen live, rather, in social orders, based upon complex systems of kinship and totemic clan loyalties, within which each man owes special allegiance to his mother's brother. These social groupings are manifested in the Papuan Gulf—as elsewhere in New Guinea—in the ways the great long houses they inhabit, or reserve for ceremonial purposes, are divided into compartments. For the men they are further stressed by the huge dugout canoes, some sixty feet long, owned communally by kin groups.

The men are chiefly concerned with head-hunting, and elaborate ritual programs from the secrets of which women are usually excluded with considerable rigor—though at times they are necessary for the fulfillment of the rituals, and are always an appreciative (and appreciated) audience of the more spectacular aspects. Nearly all aspects of ritual life involve the making and display of art objects.

In spite of the statements of earlier writers, such as the missionaries Chalmers in the 1890's and Holmes a little later, the Gulf people appear to have no pantheon of gods. The most pervasive supernatural element seems to be the quality called "imunu." The word itself is perhaps onomatopoeic, referring both to thunder and the noise made by whirling bull-roarers. The nature of imunu is not altogether clear; it is defined by Wirz (1937) as "vital strength" or "vital principal"—what gives things their own individuality. Many objects especially partake of or possess imunu, including any unusual oddment: a strangely twisted stick, for instance. On such things (which have their own names and individuality) imunu confers a special sanctity, a power, which increases with age. Probably all the ritual objects are in contact with imunu, or actually represent imunu. Some of them may indeed be condensed, so to speak, into a personification of imunu: such are the basketry animals (kaiaimunu) of the Namau.

The personified supernatural beings are generally ancestors, the great dead who retire into the bush to become its patrons and guardians, but return to be impersonated in masked ceremonies. They appear to be a somewhat generalized order of powers. The named heroes of the past seem to be exemplary, memories cherished for their achievements, but not for that reason singled out for particular reverence. The exception is the Wapo-Urama hero Irivake (Namau: Igovake), the founder of head-hunting and a lightning-spirit, who is individually represented in the ceremonial houses.

The staple food is sago, augmented by the produce of hunting, fishing, and a little cultivation of yams, taro, bananas, pineapples and other fruits. A good deal of the area's history derives from this fact. Wherever people discovered suitable sago grounds they settled and increased. Sooner or later one of the lesser groups of a community would quarrel with the others, or the ceremonial shares of feast foods would diminish through too much subdivision; then the group of malcontents would move off. In their turn they would settle in a promising spot, and the seeds of another such cycle would be planted. Thus these

9

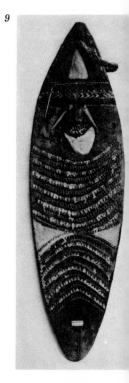

vigorous and aggressive people proliferated throughout the area in a process which has continued down to recent times.

In speaking of areas, tribes, and cultures, we must not fall into imagining that all or any of them are self-contained, in fact or even in wish. Hostility is always to be expected, but not unappeasable. An isolated stranger is in a dubious position, and may be set upon for his head; but equally he may be treated kindly and adopted. Visitors approaching a village planning to ambush them may be signalled away by friends there, while certain gestures of welcome guarantee their safety. Peace and even goodwill are practised for the sake of trade, which throws yet another network of relationships over the area. Many products are bought and used at once; some are traded again. Important commissions—such as canoes—are paid for on a royalty system until they deteriorate beyond use. The most professional business is carried on by Melanesian traders from the far eastern end of the Gulf. Every year, about the turn of September and October, they bring their great seagoing craft along the Elema coast and up the rivers of the Purari Delta. It is a three-day sail if they make good time. They stay in the Namau villages about a month, bartering their cargoes of pots and stone adzes for sago and crabs; it is estimated that perhaps 26,000 pots and 500 tons of sago have exchanged hands

in a single year. Many pots and adzes are passed on westwards. It is interesting that this trade complex does not involve ritual or ritual objects. The religious life of the Gulf seems to be quite contained in the Papuan area where, however, considerable cross-influences have occurred in the past.

8 *A Motu trading vessel sailing west. From James Chalmers, Pioneering in New Guinea, 1887. 9 Bull-roarer. Lower Fly River area. Wood, paint, 34¼" long. Cambridge 1912.791 (265)*

2 KIWAI: THE GERMINAL CULTURE

It is not possible to enter here upon a discussion of the analogies which can be traced between the Gulf cultures, the tribes just west of the Fly River, and even the Marind-anim groups. Again, the Gogodara tribe of the Aramia River (a tributary of the Bamu) has a culture related to the others of the Gulf, but an art style which, while highly self-consistent, is quite distinct from all the others.

One group, however, owns to a culture which has considerable germinal importance for the western section of the Gulf, and is felt even further eastwards. They are the people sharing a common language who live on Kiwai and other islands in the Fly River estuary, the neighboring banks of the Fly and the seacoast westwards to Mabudavane. The Kiwai islanders affirm that they are indigenous; however this may be, it is possible to see Kiwai as a junction for southwestern New Guinea, the Torres Straits, and the Gulf through which passed and were disseminated numerous ceremonial and artistic forms.

A brief account of the Kiwai culture is a useful referential framework for a description of the rest of the western Gulf.

The Kiwai subsist by agriculture, their other preoccupation being war. The ceremonial activities of these bellicose peasants are accordingly designed to promote success in fighting and fertility, which are seen as interlinked. Ceremony and magic are here virtually synonymous.

In early times, runs a Kiwai legend, there were no trees on the island; so the people lived in burrows. When at last the forests grew up, the hero Marunogere taught the people to build long houses. There are now two types: one for communal living is called moto. These huge edifices are up to thirty feet wide and hundreds of feet long. The floors are supported several feet above ground by piles; the pitched roofs are supported on four rows of towering house posts. Down each side are rows of hearths, one for each family; personal possessions are stored on racks beside and above them.

10 *Pendant figure (mimia). Lower Fly River. Wood, traces red and white paint, 13½" high. Collection Mr. and Mrs. Raymond Wielgus.*
11 *Canoe board (gope). Lower Fly River, Tirio. Coll. A. B. Lewis, 1912. Wood, paint, fibre, 37" high. Chicago 142876*

10, 11

The other houses—the darimo—are exactly similar in layout; but they are reserved entirely for the men. One end is the bush gable, used by dancers for their ceremonial entries; the other, the shore gable, is oriented to the land of the dead. When the decision to build such a house is taken, a man is asked that his old parents become "the father and mother of the darimo." He weeps, but acquiesces. The old couple take charge of the magic preparations, and oversee the gathering of many substances, all of which are war charms, to be installed under the house posts. These posts are also carved with male and female figures sometimes named after heroes. Parts of a wild pig are fastened about the building—the skull in the gable, the trotters at the corners, the vertebrae along the roof —so as to suggest it is itself a huge pig.

As the building nears completion, tension grows. The magic which has been exercised has given it a dangerous potency; it has become too "hot," and must be slaked. Strangers dare not approach the place. Sooner or later, the tribesmen organize a raid. The head of a victim is brought back, and knocked against the main house post, making the first loud sound that should be heard in the building. Now the darimo is habitable, though its power still causes visitors to faint when they enter it, and its atmosphere constantly incites the men to go head-hunting. After its completion, the father and mother inevitably die, their strength burnt out: hence their son's earlier grief.

In gardening, hunting and war, the Kiwai engage in a good deal of sympathetic magic of a sexual order; the substances gained thereby are considered to be disseminated by the swinging of bull-roarers, instruments secretly called madubu. This magical activity reaches its culmination in the great cycle of ceremonies—also instituted by Marunogere—called Moguru.* The Moguru is held once a year, and in principle consists of three main episodes. It is preceded by a number of minor rituals, games and feasts; the real business begins when boys and girls who have reached puberty are ushered into the darimo where—one sex at either end—they live for a period during which they are instructed in their coming duties as adults. From time to time they are terrorized by masked figures. They are also paired off in mock marriages which are later ratified. At another stage of the Moguru, the women enter the darimo to take part in a prolonged sexual orgy. Its purpose is the collection of semen, which is used in magic to promote the growth of the sago palms and the initiates. The most secret episode of the cycle involves the capture of a live wild boar which is carried into the darimo attired in the paint, the shell ornaments and plumed headdress of a great warrior. The young male initiates are made to crawl over its body and bite its head. The beast is highly respected for its courage and obstinacy, and (after it has been killed and eaten) parts of it are preserved for war magic. This ritual also was invented by Marunogere who, however, intended that the boar should go free; its mistaken killing by another man abolished humanity's chances of immortality.

Another cycle of ceremonies, the Mimia, is intended to harden the younger men's spirits and to ward off sickness; in it the men fight in the darimo with flaming coconut-leaf torches. These torches have first been touched to wooden images of men and women lined up along the sides of the aisle; being attached to a rope, these are made to sway in unison during the moments when the men dance. Some of these figures are nearly life-size; small ones attached to them are their "children." Other small and flat figures of men and women, also called mimia, are carried slung around the necks of the initiated, hanging on the chests of the men, down the backs of the boys: the sight is said to fill the women with joy. The large mimia figures are also carried in the prows of the war canoes on raids, and are swung towards the enemy villages so that their spirits may go ahead and weaken the opponents. In war the head is the prized trophy; only small fragments of the victim's flesh are eaten—with some revulsion—as a magical practice.

The outrigger canoes of the Fly River's banks are equipped with a sort of splashboard; the side facing inwards is carved with a human face. These boards are called gope, a word which is also the secular name of the bull-roarers. They are sometimes suspended in front of darimo gables so that they can twist in every direction, to ward off illness from whichever quarter it comes.

All of these features of the Kiwai culture should be borne in mind. The men's long house; the incidents of the Moguru ceremony; the objects—bull-roarers, masks, protective figures, boards carved with faces; the important word "gope." In the other cultures of the Gulf, all will recur in other contexts.

* Following Williams (1940) ceremonies are here given the capital letter; objects of the same name associated with them are uncapitalized. Thus: Hevehe (the ceremony); hevehe (the mask).

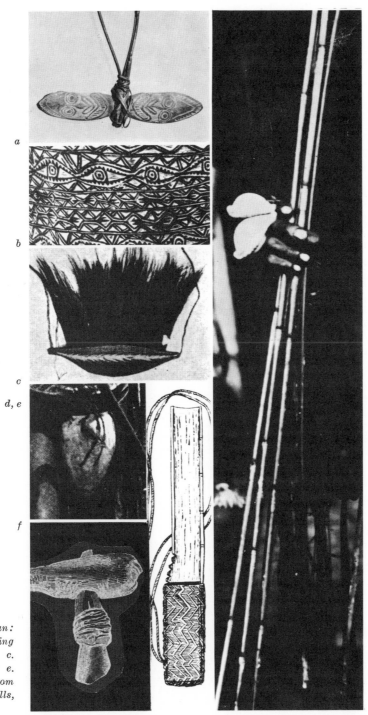

a

b

c

d, e

f

*12 Equipment of a Papuan Gulf man:
a. head carrier, Cambridge (Cowling
coll. 1909.9.1–2); b. bark belt; c.
feather headdress; d. loin shell; e.
bamboo beheading-knife; f. ax, from
Jukes 1: facing 274; g. wrist-shells,
bow and arrows*

11

3 IKO

Throughout the Gulf there are legends about many heroes. One of the greatest of these is variously named Sido in Kiwai Island; Hido along the coasts of the western Gulf; and Iko in the Purari Delta and the lands east of it.

According to the Kiwai tribes, Sido was the first to suffer death. As his body was carried home, his spirit went ahead warning the people; but they paid no attention, so he had to continue westward to Adiri, where he prepared for all mankind to follow him. He planted gardens for them; and, first transforming himself into a giant pig, he split himself open and spread out his sides to make a house several miles long.

How did Sido die? The Gope of the Wapo area tell the young initiates that Hido (as they call him) was married to his sister Hiwabu, and that they lived on an island at the mouth of the Fly River. One day, after an argument, Hiwabu went off in a temper to sit in the fork of a tree. Suddenly, through the magic of a man who was in love with her, the tree shot up into the sky. Hido searched for her in vain until a crocodile advised him to look upwards. He summoned the birds and the vine to help; none of them could reach her. Finally Hiwabu called that he should go to Neuri Hill, near the Kikori River. Hido set out, chopping down trees as he went with his stone axe, crossing the rivers in his path: the Bamu, the Gama, the Turama. When he reached Neuri, he found that Hiwabu's tree had landed at the village of a man called Aiburu. After making a big feast and fighting with Aiburu, Hido took Hiwabu away, this time to Kiwai.

The Purari Delta people say Iko was one of several heroes who came out of the west to teach them important matters. Iko himself travelled from Urama (or even beyond) to Vaimuru; he brought with him the secrets of masked ceremonies and the drum which was his twin brother. Moreover, he even taught the original ancestor of the Vaimuru people, who lived in an underground shelter, how to make a house, and gave this man's descendants the rules which govern marriage and kinship.

Both the Purari people and the Elema tribes say that Iko was made welcome at first, then rejected. The hero was the victor in a struggle with his wife's lover, whose followers, however, killed him in revenge and devoured his body. As his uncle sat mourning in the men's house, his uneaten share of the flesh at his side, a wonder!—he saw the resurrected Iko enter and walk down the length of the building. But Iko was murdered a second time, and a third; then he finally left the land of the living for the land of the dead in the west, as his uncle recited a farewell:

"Your bow, your bag, your belt; your pearl shell, arm shell, feathers; your loin band, axe, knife, dog's teeth—these your things, take them and go, your ornaments and property."

4 THE KEREWA CULTURE OF THE WEST

14 Long house at Buniki, Bamu River, May 30, 1845. From Jukes, 1:273. 15, 16 Ancestral board (gope-kaiaimunu), per-

Hido's path was taken at some unknown historic time by many bands of emigrants from Kiwai Island. They found a low-lying country of wide estuaries and small islands as they went eastwards to the Bamu, the Turama and the Omati; to the Kikori with Goaribari Island at its mouth; and further east still to Urama Island. Near the sea the muddy riverbanks, low to sea level, hemmed in with mangrove, hardly resist the terrifying bores sweeping in at the full and new moons; further upstream and on the islands are belts of game-stocked sago forests and scrub. The rain falls here constantly from the overcast skies. From just beyond the Turama River and on into the delta of the Purari, the country is a labyrinth of narrow waterways cutting through a wilderness of jungle swamp.

Seminomadic bush tribes were originally in unstable possession of the area: the Tamayi east of the Bamu River, who had originally migrated from the neighborhood of Mount Leonard Murray; and the various divisions of the Kasere between the Turama and the Omati, and to the east of the Omati.

When the westerners came, Kiwai-speaking and Waboda people apparently settled the west bank of the Bamu, and the islands at its mouth. Several of the six Turamarubi tribes established themselves up the Turama River, past the estuarine Baru people; others remained at its mouth on the large Morigi Island. One Fly River group moved in several recorded stages, starting from Auti, on Kiwai Island, to Keme at the mouth of the Omati River. Some of the Keme people then moved on to Vaimuru in the Purari Delta, apparently by way of Urama, and later proliferated into the Kaimari tribe of the Namau group. Still other Keme people founded Kerewa on Goaribari Island; and Kerewa is acknowledged as the parent village of several settlements on the mainland as well as Goaribari itself. Heroes, speaking the Kiwai dialect (called Kerewa wadi), indeed appear in legend as bearers of a culture to the whole area —no doubt justly. The Gope and the Iwaino of Urama claimed, in fact, that their hero Irivake taught the Kasere all they knew of civilization. Many native groups adopted much of the speech and customs of Kerewa, or, like the Paiya, split with their indigenous Kasere stock. If they were not originally of

sonal name Baiyau. Kerewa area. Coll. P. Wirz, 1930. Wood, paint, fibre tassels, 67½" high. Collection Mr. Serge Brignoni

Kiwai stock, the Turamarubi took on Kerewa culture. Even some Purari Delta groups moved into the Kerewa circle of influence, and others which did not so move were affected by it.

At all events, the area around Goaribari Island became, and is, the richest in the western Gulf, both in terms of population and the development of culture. All in all, there are between twenty and thirty thousand people in the area, 12,000 of them speaking the Kerewa dialect. Goaribari itself acts as middleman in trade from east and west.

None of these events can be dated, of course, though a Kiwai tradition would seem to place the foundation of Auti sometime after 1840—probably much too recent. All this surely happened before 1845, when a party from HMS "Fly" made the first recorded landing on May 30. The Englishmen observed two major elements of the culture: the long houses and the collections of head-hunting trophies. After some opposition from the tribesmen, the explorers entered a vacated long house at "Pigville"—probably Buniki on the Bamu River—during one of the downpours typical of the region. They helped themselves to pigs and other property, including several decorated trophy skulls: thefts which were remembered against them nearly fifty years afterwards.

The villages here are of somewhat different layout from those of Kiwai, and considerable mythology attaches to the houses. Among the Turamarubi it is said that the first mother of mankind was a sow called Wimaio who bore true men and women. They lived in trees until the sow showed them how to make communal long houses (Turama: darimo, Kerewa: dubu daima), though another legend says this was done by a man from Kerewa called Kopepamu. The sow divided the people into six clans. Because of this, the Turama long houses are parcelled into three sections: the bush end, the middle, and the salt-water end. They have verandahs at each end, and half a dozen side entrances. Their interiors are divided into cubicles at these entrances, marking out the areas allotted to the several clans. At the mouth of the Bamu, but perhaps not elsewhere, the main house posts are carved with images of heroes, as they are in Kiwai. These houses are the preserves of the married men; the junior men have smaller, analogous buildings. The private dwellings, in which the women live, are ranged along the sides of the ceremonial house and sometimes connected to it by gangplanks.

The ritual mainspring of the area's culture consists of a form of the Kiwai Moguru, to which the Gulf people have assimilated their own form of the head-hunting raid, and an intensive practice of cannibalism. The capture of a head is the validating act which rounds off the completion of such important group undertakings as housebuilding, canoemaking, and initiations: at Ubua a beheaded corpse is drained of its blood over a new canoe. The legs and arms of victims, usually bush tribesmen, are eaten with frank enjoyment.

The main purpose of the Moguru ceremony in Kiwai is the making of garden magic; but from the Bamu to the Kerewa area the stress is on the revelation to boys and girls of the secrets of adult sexual life. Indeed, while no doubt the various activities may in practice be performed at will, the episodes of Moguru and raid may ideally be a single extended ritual sequence; and several types of masks and wooden carvings are brought into play for its fulfilment. The carvings include what may loosely be called ancestral tablets; others known as agiba to which skulls are attached; and figures made specially for exhibition to the initiates. All these are also revered during the quotidian spells between the major ceremonies.

The ancestral tablets—tall, oval boards carved in relief outlining human figures, and painted—exist in three classes, a division particularly marked among the Kerewa groups. Usage in naming these seems to vary from place to place—available evidence is somewhat conflicting—but among the Kerewa they are apparently collectively called gope; kaiaimunu; or titi-ebiha (carved/ornamented–crocodile/guardian –spirit). The most sacred examples are sometimes called darimo (daimowa)-ebiha. Each clan group owns one of these large boards, which is stored under the roof of the men's house, is never taken out of it, and has a certain aura of secrecy. Every six years or so, in connection with initiations, the darimo-ebiha is burned and a new one is made, being inaugurated by the taking of a head. Less important and less endowed with spiritual power are the smaller, individually owned boards

17   18

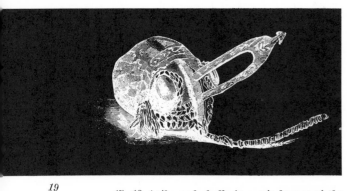

19

17, 18 Agiba and skulls in men's houses of the Kerewa area, 1930. 19 Trophy skull from Buniki, Bamu River. Coll. HMS "Fly" expedition, 1845. Formerly Royal College of Surgeons, destroyed in air raid, World War II. From Jukes, 1:opp.274. 20 Trophy skulls mounted on sticks on the foreshore at Goaribari

apparently called obina-ebiha; they stand at the entrances to the clan cubicles, and are inaugurated with pigs. Both darimo-ebiha and obina-ebiha also have individual names, after ancestors and places. Boys and young uninitiated men own small, unnamed boards, which are hung in the cubicles or on the outside walls of their houses; these are supposed to help the growth of the boys, losing potency after the initiations. The gope boards are, among other functions, protective beings who ward off sickness and other ills; early European visitors to the Kerewa villages were met on the shore by crowds of men waving palm branches and gope. As for their origin, the Kerewa people say that their ancestors reached Keme without any gope but that Baiyau—the most important one—travelled after them from Kiwai under the earth, followed by all the others. Bearing in mind the canoe-gope of the Fly River, it is clear that, strictly speaking, they are not a Kerewa invention. On the other hand it is also probable that their evaluation is a Kerewa development, as such boards seem to be more highly regarded by them than by any other Gulf culture. Even in this western area, they are apparently less important on the Turama, and absent from the Bamu tribes. In some sense they are probably surrogates for the bull-roarer, which is unknown in this area.

At Dopima (on Goaribari Island) the main ceremonial cycle is called Gibumamu, and apparently incorporates the Moguru (Buguru). It begins one day at sunrise; the children are ushered into the ceremonial house by their mothers' brothers, who act as sponsors. A shelter of sago-palm leaves, built inside the main hall at the salt-water end, is hung with the gope, a row of skulls from the agiba lying on the floor before

16

them. The young initiates are seated in a row in front of these sacred objects; the sponsors, lined up between skulls and gope, sing to the accompaniment of drum music. The gope are travelling underground, they sing; the gope are rising up from below in their desire to kill enemies; the gope are enraged if their names are not called; the agiba are watching the feather ornaments of the gope bob about as they are carried. This lasts all day and into the night; next morning the children are ritually washed and go into seclusion, but the singing continues for the two to six months the cycle lasts.

Among the initiatory ceremonies is one in which the children straddle dead pigs. A feast is held when this initiatory period ends. The gope are brought back into the main hall to the singing of their songs. When all of them are ranged in their proper positions, the sponsors dance through the building holding their gope at arm's length, each initiate clinging to a string tied in one of the board's perforations.

By early evening the house is dark. The sponsors silently take positions along the walls, their initiates at their sides, small torches burning in the upper perforations of the gope held in front of them. Equally silently, men from neighboring villages enter with their drums; so do the women. Finally, the village headman enters with his wife, beating a bunch of leaves on his thigh. When he reaches the leader of the feast there is a great outburst of drumming and shouts, and a flare of torchlight; a dance begins which culminates in an orgy.

In the morning the gope are carried outside. The headman calls the roll of enemy villages until the gope stir in the bearers' hands: the sign of which should be raided. They are laid face downward on the ground until evening, when they are re-installed. Next day the raid is launched, as the gope spirits have already gone ahead to sap the strength of the prospective victims—as do those of the mimia figures of Kiwai.

Masks (made of plaited rattan) are used during these initiations, but their functions are not altogether clear. One type, from Kerewa, the Turama, and the Bamu is a round and dome-shaped head with a long pointed nose; it is called kauvai, and on the Bamu represents some mythical character. On the Turama and in Kerewa there is another type of mask, also round but with a long loop for a nose, called kavai. This is also, in Kerewa, called avoko: a name it shares with a type of dance headdress in the shape of a long house. This long house headdress recalls a Purari Delta funerary ceremony in which a model house is displayed in procession.

One episode of the initiatory ritual consists of the exhibition to the young initiates of sacred images of human beings and animals. At Torobina on the Bamu River, for instance, (where, as on the Turama River, they may be of great size) these are specifically carvings of men; a woman; a crocodile; a shark; a pig; and a pigeon. In general these figures are revealed to the children on the last night of the Moguru, some of them tied to the central post of the ceremonial house, others lying on the floor surrounded by the captured trophy heads and, recently, the carved substitutes for these.

Normally these skulls, decorated with seeds, shells, and rattan or carved wooden loops in their noses, are attached by loops from the jaws to the numerous agiba boards which embellished every men's house, heaped on a small shelf in front of it. An agiba is a silhouette half-length figure with two long,

20

vertical projections between the arms and the torso—the projections being the supports for the skulls. Each clan has its agiba in its own compartment of the long house: sometimes they are paired, when the larger is the male, the smaller the female. There can be no doubt of their importance and sanctity, when one considers the crucial role of head-hunting in the culture, especially in its relation to fertility.

The Turamarubi claim to have obtained them first from the bush tribes (Tamayi) between the Bamu and the Turama; the cult spread south over the whole area from the Bamu to Goaribari. When this took place is unknown. Jukes, writing about the "Fly" expedition, speaks of the skulls hanging on a sort of frame, but does not mention any carving. However, darkness and unfamiliarity may have prevented his seeing such an object even had it been there. Small carvings of the same design are made throughout the area for the skulls of small animals, fish and birds. Some of these are even found in Kiwai.

An agiba is carved by a man when he has taken a head, and other men hang the skulls of their victims and (possibly) relatives on it. On the completion of a ceremonial house, it is customary to kill and eat a stranger in the building; this was the occasion for the murder of James Chalmers at Dopima in 1901. During the punitive raid that followed, twenty such houses were burned, but not before over 700 skulls had been counted on the agiba in one, and some 400 in another.

The agiba is primed to receive each captured head by being repainted by an old man, the "father of the agiba." Until then it is harmless; afterwards, as is true of other wooden carvings, it becomes imbued with sanctity, with "heat."

21, 22, 23 Drums. Kerewa area. Wood, paint. Amsterdam 2670.371, 2670.372, 2670.375. 24, 25 Interiors of men's ceremonial houses, Wapo-Era district, 1930

Small carvings of human figures (also called agiba in the Kerewa area) are also associated with the skulls, and kept near them. Some, apparently of the same type, were actually carried on head-hunting expeditions to make the canoes invisible. They were also ancestral representations, carved for and given to the children of dead men and women.

A series of dances to celebrate success in head-hunting, developed by the Baru, was also taken over by the Turamarubi. In the Turama cycle, a ritual friend of the successful head-hunter cleans the skull, decorates it, carves a stick on which it is carried and gives it offerings of food. The feasts and dances, taking place at intervals over several months, mark various payments made by the killer for these services. They end with one as a climax to which all the heads taken by the tribe are

24   25

mounted on their sticks outside the men's house. The dances are accompanied by songs full of erotic implications: the dancers sing that the house should rock with their dancing, that their ornaments should sway with their movements:

"Sway wonderful scarlet flower
  Sway long house like a scarlet flower in the breeze
  Scarlet flower from the land of the dead
  Wonderful scarlet flower from the land of the dead where
    flowers are like a hand dipped in blood
  The arm shell sways like feathers in the hair
  The carved bark belt sways
  The dracaenas knock against the dancers answering the call
    of the dracaenas worn in the back of their belts."

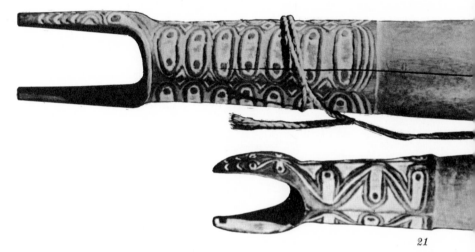

21

22

23

5 WAPO, URAMA, AND THE ERA RIVER

To the west of the Kerewa area lies a further complex of islands bounded on the east by the Era River, which also sets a limit to the Purari Delta. On Urama Island, in the Era's mouth; around Wapo Creek, which flows into Era Bay; and on the Era River itself are cultures which both show the influence of their neighbors and share characteristics of their own.

The culture of Wapo Creek, where the leading group is the Gope, has men's houses divided with partitions into clan cubicles opening onto a central aisle. The head-hunting trophies are displayed here in a strikingly different arrangement from that of the western Gulf. The upper parts of the partitions are grills, with a skull fixed into each aperture. By the skulls hang small wooden figures: and these, in this area, go by the name agiba. The lower parts of the partitions are sheathed in bark slabs; in front of them stand the gope boards. (Their alternative name—kaiaimunu—is applied to the bull-roarers.) In front of the gope again, on the floor, lie the pig and crocodile skulls; each of these is straddled by a smaller type of flat silhouette figure (bioma), or another type (kakame) made of a natural branch, the legs being inserted in the eye sockets.

The same order is observed in Urama (among the Iwaino) and in the Era River region, with the difference that in these two areas the agiba are considerably fewer but the gope far more profuse, both in number and variety of their designs. The western type of hook agiba appears only in isolated examples, which merely stand on the floor among the gope.

Throughout the area, pairs of large figures are found in the men's houses. Some are constructed of various materials; others, of wood, resemble outsize agiba figures. These are direct representations of the hero Irivake, who founded head-hunting. Apart from this major achievement, Irivake was also, as has been mentioned, a disseminator of culture to the bush people; and climbed to the sky and controls the lightning.

Kanipu masks (as rounded heads with long open jaws) occur in the Era district. Apparently they are worn by young boys during initiations. A corselet surmounted with a long neck crowned with a small head—this costume is huge in Urama, smaller in other districts—is used to enforce the tabu on coconuts destined for use in ceremonies. Most striking of all is a type which does not occur to the west. Here they are called keweke: tall, flat, oval forms with protruding jaws at the lower end. They are made of basketry (clayed and painted in the Era district; but in Wapo and Urama covered with bark cloth) with designs outlined in applied strips of rattan, filled in with color. These keweke masks vary in size, being ten or twelve feet high in Urama, but considerably less in Wapo and the Era district.

An important difference between Wapo and Urama, and the Era district, is found in the form of the men's houses. In the first two, these are long buildings with more or less level roof lines, probably open at one end and screened at the other, with only a small entrance. In Wapo and Urama women may, and indeed on ceremonial occasions must, enter the men's houses. In the Era not only are women strictly excluded, but the actual shape of the house is different: it tapers and decreases in height towards the back, and there is no rear entrance. This is because shrines at the far end house kaiaimunu in yet another form: huge animal-like creatures made of basketry. The bull-roarers are stored inside them, and their sound represents the creatures' voices. These basketry animals, and their mythological and ritual significance, are an important feature in the culture of the Purari Delta.

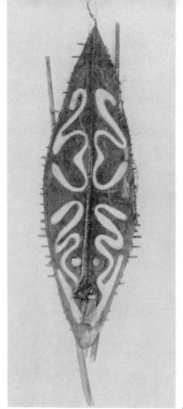

26

26 Mask (keweke). Wapo-Era district. Coll. P. Wirz 1930. 65⅜" high. Basel Vb 1198. 27 Kaiaimunu animals in an Era River men's house, 1930. 28 Maipua village, May 1912

27

6 THE PURARI DELTA NAMAU TRIBES

The Namau (as they are called by their neighbors, the Elema) live in the delta formed by the five mouths of the Purari River. The easternmost is the Aivei River—the Namau's lands are bounded by its west bank—and then successively westwards the Panaroa, the Urika, the Baroi, and the Wame which empties into the Kapaina or Pie River. Their far western border is the Era River, though they have a few villages on its further side. These large waterways are connected by a network of smaller streams which extends over about five hundred square miles of swampland. Here again, little is above sea level; from time to time huge expanses are under floodwater. However the Namau live abundantly by hunting and fishing, and, since the delta is one of the richest sago-producing areas of the whole coast, can trade a large surplus to the visiting Melanesians.

Altogether there are about eight to nine thousand Namau; they consider themselves as divided into four tribes. Along the coast live the Kaimari, who migrated from Urama Island, in Kaimari itself, Vaimuru and Maipua. The Koriki claim to be the delta's indigenous inhabitants, and live in the parent village of Ukiravi and seven others.

The Iari, named after their principal village but also settled in three others, inhabit the eastern delta; the Baroi have four villages in the northwest hinterland. All these communities live on terms of enmity or friendship with each other, which seem mostly to be governed by considerations of the distance which lends enchantment to the view. Neighbors are almost invariably at odds; perhaps deliberately so, to preserve head-hunting facilities.

The big villages, built along the riverbanks, consist of private houses which are pile dwellings up to a hundred feet long. They have pitched roofs perhaps thirty or forty feet high at the front peak, and both slanting down and narrowing

towards the rear. Inside they are subdivided into as many separate areas, each with its own hearth, as the owner has wives. The Namau call the men's ceremonial houses ravi: of the same general appearance as the private houses but about double the size. These houses are quite numerous: in Ukiravi there were as many as eight at a time, besides three smaller ones intended for the use of young boys.

Chalmers, probably the first European to enter a ravi, described (1887) the interior of one at Iari (or Ravi Kivau) in 1883: "I looked down an aisle nearly two hundred feet in length. All down either side was hung with what looked like splendid silk curtains, and these were made from the young frond of the sago palm split up when quite new. The flooring of the aisle, two feet broad, appeared to be a dark-stained, highly polished wood, and carved with figures of men, crocodiles, and cassowaries [also footprints and eye-designs]; this was made from the skin of the sago palm and received its high polish from the blood of victims dragged along to the end...."

At Ukiravi, among the Koriki, Igovake (Irivake) is represented by pairs of effigies on each side of the ravi entrance. These are seven-foot cones of packed sago, swathed in palm leaves with coconut heads. They are eaten by the old men on the first appearance of the kanipu masks.

The interior of the ravi is divided into a series of cubicles, opening off the central aisle. Each cubicle is a larava, and the group of men who use it as a home away from home goes by the same name. The partitions separating each larava are hung with that group's kwoi boards, similar to the gope of the Wapo-Urama district. They are owned by individuals, and form part of fathers' legacies to their sons. Here too the kwoi—though many are merely decorations—have some relationship to the trophy skulls of men, pigs and crocodiles which are stacked at the foot of the partition; they also have a vague connection with the kaiaimunu.

The kaiaimunu are the holiest things known to the Namau, and are kept in the partitioned-off rear section (ravi oru) of the building. They are huge four-legged beasts with gaping jaws,

29 30

29 Head (imunu). Purari Delta. Wood scorched black, red and white paint. Coll. P. Wirz, 1930. 15¾" long. Basel Vb 7912. 30 Figure (imunu). Purari Delta, Ikinu. Wood, 46" long. Amsterdam 2670.303. Interiors of men's ceremonial houses at: 31 Maipua; 32, 33 Kairu; May 1912

31 32

constructed of wickerwork; they are up to twelve feet long and seven feet high. Each has across its brow a roll-shaped ornament, the "thunder-cloud"; chiefs wear this when conducting war parties. When new, the beasts are decked out with red seed eyes, feathers and crotons. Generally speaking they are left quite alone; Chalmers describes seeing them in their shelter with swarms of small bats flitting in and out of their great mouths. Only the old men dare approach them.

The wickerwork beasts are not vaguely possessed of "imunu," as are the oddments known by that name. They are the actual imunu. According to the Vaimuru people, they were brought to the Namau by Iko. The Koriki believe they were revealed to mankind by Iri and Kai, the mythical ancestors who founded Ukiravi. These two had no house, so they built the first kaiaimunu to live in, flooring it with bull-roarers. This was Eamu. After a time they learned to build a proper ravi—Kairi Mai—into which they moved Eamu, where it remains to this day. Later on men went out from Kairi Mai to found the other ravis of the Purari Delta. Now every larava (in theory at least) has an individual kaiaimunu with its own name. While the kaiaimunu live in the ravi, their spirits may sometimes leave the building to haunt the rivers with which each (like its larava) is associated. Each is also associated with a stated animal, probably most often a fish, which is its "canoe." But above all, they are extraordinarily potent beings, expressing their will through dreams and thunder, who should be placated with offerings of food from day to day.

Initiation into other cults is more or less optional, but every male goes through Pairama, initiation to the kaiaimunu. This begins with the seclusion of the young boys in the ravi, where the older men feed them well and entertain them with songs. After some months of this, the whole group goes off to the bush to gather cane. Then the old kaiaimunu are brought out of hiding and placed in their respective larava. A boy is lifted onto each figure, the frail wickerwork collapsing under his weight. The boys help the men to build new kaiaimunu, thus revivifying and renewing the power and energy of the patron

beings. After this the boys are carried about the ravi in the monsters' mouths.

Bull-roarers are the focus of a special cult. They are called upura or imunu viki, a phrase which means "weeping imunu" —when they are sounded at a chief's death, the imunu is lamenting over him. If anything they are more potent and dangerous than the kaiaimunu, and even more secret. Comparatively few men acquire the distinctions of being initiated into the knowledge of their existence and use, and of owning one. Even their possessors will not handle them any more than is strictly necessary.

Masks in the making or ready for use are suspended from the ravi roof. Although there are several types, most go by the general name of aiaimunu. The commonest type is the tall, flat oval with long projecting jaws. Those of Koriki itself are almost round, and quite small. The aiaimunu represent spirits of the bush, and their name may possibly mean "drum imunu." Most are anonymous; only about half a dozen are important enough to have names of their own. Their ritual is a series of appearances and parades (Aiau) which are comparatively modest in ceremony and consumption of time. They are an assertion of the reality of the spirits for the edification of the women.

A type of small, round mask (kanipu) is used to enforce a tabu on coconuts which will be used in feasts, and the wearer haunts the groves bearing arms. Like the western Gulf tribes from which they stem, the Kaimari group have a type of mask called avoko; in their case a face-mask with a bulbous brow. They also have abo-abo ("crazy") masks which are conical with winglike side projections.

The final episode of all such ceremonies is the hunt for a human offering—a gope. Here the kaiaimunu is resorted to for oracles. When the party is assembled on the water, they wait to set out until the kaiaimunu rocks the canoes; then they move off in the direction which the kaiaimunu has indicated by piling up thunderclouds above it.

Although the Namau tribes sometimes fight pitched battles in which dozens of canoes are engaged, the usual quarry of a head-hunt is some isolated stranger, man, woman or child. The hunters return to the village rattling their paddles against the sides of their canoes as a signal of success. On their arrival they run with the body to the ravi, down its length, and into the ravi oru. They cram either the head or the whole body into the kaiaimunu, which is made to bound with joy then spit it out upon the ravi floor. There it lies for the night.

In the evening the men parade through the building with torches. The killer hands his to his wife, who has been waiting outside. She takes to her heels pursued by any man who desires her, being paid later for her services with arm shells. Such is the Koriki practice; in Kaimari (with its western affiliations) the equivalent is an orgy, involving unmarried girls, on the war party's return. The following day the killer is carried in triumph through the village standing in a canoe.

Meanwhile, anyone who wishes has been free to help himself to such part of the corpse as he fancies eating. This is generally effected without ceremony; however, sometimes and in some places, it is said, the bodies are hacked up with bull-roarers for distribution. Cannibalism, the Namau claim, was introduced by the Urama immigrants at Kaimari. A legend describes how

33

the Namau used to eat certain large fish under the impression that they were men. Aua Makua, a hero from the west, corrected their mistake by laying out his raid victims on the ravi floor with the words, "These are your real gope!" (Oddly enough it was the Kaimari-related village of Maipua which first abandoned cannibalism. The story goes that after the Elema came under government protection, the little boys of Orokolo found themselves in the delightful position of being able to deride Maipua visitors, for being man-eaters, with complete impunity. Frustrated from taking revenge on Orokolo in old-fashioned style, the Maipua retaliated in a typically Papuan way: they ostentatiously gave up cannibalism. Their Kaimari kinsmen followed suit in sympathy, as later did the rest of the Namau.)

After a series of successful head-hunts, "gope" makes a final appearance as the name of a masque in which men dressed in costumes of palm-leaf mats perform a buffoonish dance. At Maipua at least they are said to be the spirits of the slain and eaten dead. They have to be avoided, as the touch of their mud-covered hands brings illness.

34   35

Just across the Namau frontier formed by the Aivei River, there begins a belt of fertile country which borders the Gulf for eighty miles. This is backed by hills infested by the dreaded Kukukuku, cannibalistic mountaineers, while a stretch of barren coast on the east sets a natural barrier between the Melanesian people of the end of the island and the Papuans of the Gulf itself.

Along the shore live about twelve tribes, grouped together under the general name "Elema" by the Motuan traders. According to their own legends, they migrated from an original home back in the foothills, and near the east bank of the Purari River. As they came down to the coast the Pairavu tribe, living behind what is now Orokolo, barred their way; so some continued straight down the Purari to the sea, while others bore eastwards, crossed the Vailala River, and settled at different points along the shore. Holmes thinks that the Moreaipi reached the coast about 1800, the Toaripi, who live farthest east, about 1850; but Haddon believes this is putting it much too late (Haddon & Hornell, 2:207). At any rate the Moreaipi

34 Interior of men's ceremonial house at Vailala with shields, hohao and masks; 35 Interior of a boy's ceremonial house with kovave masks Vailala. April–May 1912

were displaced from their original settlements by the Maipua, and moved to Orokolo.

The Elema are distinct in many customs from the western Gulf people. Thus, while they are head-hunters, they look upon cannibalism with extreme repugnance. They are more or less monogamous. They are even physically different, being taller and lighter-skinned than the Namau and other tribes of the area.

The large Elema villages are composed of groups of hamlets strung out a little way back from the shore line, the most striking buildings being the huge ceremonial houses (eravo). These may be a hundred feet long, rising to a fifty-foot peak at the front, but no more than twelve feet high at the back. In the Elema villages the men's eravo faces the sea; the boys' eravos face inland.

The Elema do not partition off the eravo into cubicles; only the great pairs of house posts mark the divisions of the laravas. Nor is there a sacred area at the end, which merely opens on a verandah. But here too, carved wooden tablets (hohao), though not in large numbers, figure among the house's furnishings. These as usual represent faces, and sometimes (in Vailala) full figures. Engraved dwarf coconuts (marupai, sorcerer's charms) are often suspended from their noses. A few figures in the round are also called hohao in Orokolo. Possibly they are the equivalent of paired figures, called semese, found in the western Elema men's houses. Some of the hohao boards, being recognized as merely decorative, have no names. Those which are named are sacred; they represent bush spirits which indeed inhabit them and may sometimes emerge to wander about the eravo. The named tablets are also called kaiavuru—a word which may certainly be equated with "kaiaimunu."

Among the most important social divisions of the Elema are ten or so patrilineal groups called aualari. Differently named from place to place, they are connected with ancestors and totems, and each has its own carefully conserved set of myths: the mythology of the Elema is indeed notable for its richness and the almost inordinate length of the legends.

The Elema tribes share among them three main cults: those of the bull-roarer, the spirits of the bush, and the spirits of the sea. The cult of the bull-roarers (also called kaiavuru) is believed to be the oldest; in any case, these extremely sacred objects are kept well out of sight in carefully wrapped bundles. Bull-roarers have no spectacular ceremonies connected with them; on the other hand, the cults of sea spirits (Hevehe) and bush spirits (Kovave) are celebrated with elaborate pageantry, the greater of the two being that of the sea spirits. We have very full records of these observances among the western Elema of Orokolo Bay (Williams, 1940).

The western Elema think of the Kovave as mythical, superhuman beings of past ages who now live in trees. The ceremonies are designed to summon them from their homes, to feast them when they have come, and to initiate boys into the cult. The proceedings begin with the construction in the eravo of the conical masks also called kovave; when they are completed, they are smuggled away to a clearing in the bush. The young novices are led in that direction by their uncles, and are suddenly surprised by a rush of men from ambush to clap the masks over their heads. As Kovave, they make a formal entry into the village next day, and take up residence in the eravo. During the following month they patrol the beach daily—half-menacing, half-entertaining figures—and are presented ceremonially with pigs, which they slaughter with their arrows. Eventually, the Kovave retire to the bush where the initiates impersonating them are divested of the masks, which are then burned. The eastern Elema know Kovave under several different names: Harisu, Haruhu, Harihu; or Oio and Oioi.

It may be mentioned here that farther west, among the Toaripi at Motumotu, are a few types of otherwise unrecorded masks; nothing is known of their significance. The first type is a huge construction worn by dancers in sets. The mask apparently represents a horizontal animal head, with a three-pronged crest at the back rising as high as fifteen or twenty feet. It is as though the mouthpiece of the hevehe-semese-aiamunu masks were exaggerated, the upper panel being remodelled. The second type of mask is an animal head; and a third is little more than a snouted cap.

The great sea spirit cycle is based on a belief in vast legendary monsters living in Orokolo Bay and the nearby river mouths. They are the ma-hevehe; accordingly, the ceremonial cycle is called Hevehe. There seems to be a mystical connection between the ma-hevehe and the bull-roarers: in legend, the monster Oa Birakapu terrorized the Elema until he was killed by mercenaries from the Purari; while they were cutting up his body, the Namau women found the first bull-roarer (and the hevehe and kovave masks) in the entrails. The hevehe masks are long oval forms with jaws, like the aiaimunu masks of the Namau; and Williams suggests that they are in effect representations of huge bull-roarers; that those who wear them are "dancing bull-roarers bearing drums."

Versions of this cycle appear throughout the Elema tribes under different names and with a different significance, but always with the tall oval masks. The eastern Elema call it Sevese or Semese—words said to mean "the warriors," though taken by earlier writers to be the name of a god. Among the Karama the masks represent ancestral spirits, and the whole ceremony celebrates their return to the village to be placated with gifts. If they are returning from the bush, then we can draw a comparison between the Elema's Semese and the

Namau's Aiau; as well as Semese's being a senior version of Kovave. This seems to point up the importance and profundity of the recent changes effected in the meaning of Hevehe among the western Elema.

The Hevehe cycle begins in Orokolo when the members of an eravo perform a brief and fairly casual ceremony in which a coconut is split in two and a little magic is made. But this launches what will become a major effort of the whole community, lasting moreover anything from ten to twenty years. This is partly because work is sporadic. Not only must large numbers of huge masks be constructed; wealth must be acquired and pigs fattened to provide for numerous feasts, and payments be made for various privileges, which enliven the community and stimulate its economic life. Furthermore, mourning, quarrels and sorcery may all hold up the proceedings for indefinitely prolonged periods. In theory, the building of an eravo inaugurates a Hevehe cycle, and the whole cycle should be carried out from it; in practice the invariable delays mean that a cycle is likely to outwear several eravo.

The first important act of the Hevehe cycle is an expedition into the bush to cut loops of cane for the framework of the first two masks. These are brought into the eravo on a moonless night, after the women have been warned indoors. A crowd of men—shouting, sounding shell trumpets and drums—swarms along the beach to the eravo, then back the way they came. The purpose of this demonstration is to carry in the cane; it symbolizes the visit of a ma-hevehe from the sea bringing with him two of his daughters, whom he leaves in the care of the men. Time and again the monster visits his children, bringing others to keep the first pair company, and ornaments for all of

 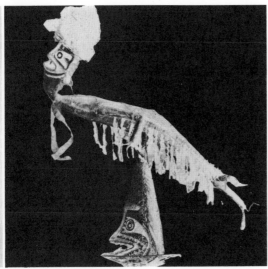

36 Mask (eharo). Orokolo. Coll. before 1913. Cane; bark cloth; fiber; leaves; red, black and white paint; 56" high. QM E.13/245. 37 Mask (kovave). Coll. before 1890. Cane, bark cloth, paint, 35" high. Dublin 332.90. 38 Mask (eharo). Orokolo. Coll. before 1913. Cane; bark cloth, fiber; leaves; red, black and white paint; 49½" high. QM E.13/215. 36 and 38 from Harris, 1913

them; and each of these occasions is marked by the acting-out of the ma-hevehe's turbulent invasions of the village from the sea.

The masks are constructed in the eravo. They belong to the aualari groups; so do the patterns representing totemic objects worked on them. Sometimes the same design is used by more than one aualari, in which case it will be named differently from group to group and be said to represent different objects. The masks themselves also have traditional aualari names, and thereby offer to the knowledgeable innumerable references to the myths of his group. At the same time, any man may make his own mask and name it on the inspiration of his dreams or supernatural experiences; as with the hohao, some of these names are secret magic.

When the masks are nearly finished a new door is installed in the eravo. This is the occasion for an important ceremony during the festivities; still another type of mask—the eharo—makes its appearance. The eharo masks are generally conical (like kovave) but carry models of totemic creatures which are lightly constructed, so that the wings of birds, or the leaves of trees, wave and stir with the movements of the dancers. Some eharo represent mythological characters, often with comic personalities. Perhaps at one time the eharo were considered as bush spirits: there is even some evidence that they were still taken very seriously at the turn of this century. Recently, however, they have been considered as merely entertaining side shows. One may also mention here a type of round mask with a bulging forehead which is perhaps an eharo, but resembles the western kanipu in form.

Eventually, the ma-hevehe's daughters are ready to emerge from the seclusion of the eravo in which they have been sheltered for so many years. Through the night of tense anticipation which precedes this, the Revelation, the village women dance. Early in the morning, the shell trumpets sound from the eravo, and the ma-hevehe answers the signal by coming up from the sea for the last time, carrying drums for his children. For several hours the men beat the drums in the ceremonial house, while the women standing outside call on the hevehe to show themselves. Finally they respond as Williams (1940) describes:

"It was still dusk, nearly an hour before sunrise, and the tall front of Avavu Ravi hardly more than a black outline against the sky, when they began to open the door. But in the course of years the eravo had canted to the right, so that it had been necessary to prop it with heavy posts on one side and guy it with lawyer vines on the other. The 30-foot door had consequently jammed, and though the lashings had been severed, there was now some difficulty in opening it. A number of men standing on the ground to the left front of the building hauled on the lawyer vines attached to the farther edge of the door, but while it began to come clear at the bottom, it still stuck at the top corner. The women's cries had died away and a hush of expectancy had fallen over the crowd of watchers.... Several men sprang up the scaffolding of the *kora papaita* for a better purchase.... One of the climbers, a splendid, powerful figure, reached the topmost rung and in that precarious position threw his whole weight onto the line. At that, with a rending of wood and bamboo, the topmost corner was released and the eravo door swung open. Even as it did so the first of the hevehe was standing on the threshold.

"There are many dramatic situations in the cycle, but none can compare with this supreme moment when the hevehe, after well-nigh twenty years of confinement, issue forth to commence the brief fulfillment of their existence. In the grey light of early morning the first of them, 'Koraia,' stood framed against the blackness of the open door—a tall fantastic figure, silvery white, its colored patterns in the atmosphere of dawn appearing pale and very delicate. The garishness, the grotesquerie, that full daylight and a near view might discover were now blurred; they faded into something fairylike. One of the spirits—of forest, sea, or air—one of the Magic People, one of the Immortal Story Folk, was about to lead its companions out of their long immurement to dance and make merry in the village. A strange, otherworldly figure, and a heathenish one, no doubt; but none who saw it poised on that dark threshold could have failed to call it beautiful.

"For a brief moment 'Koraia' stood there, the great crowd of spectators gazing in silence. Then, with a thump of the drum and a prodigious rattling of harau [seed anklets], it started down the gangway. Immediately behind it came 'Pekeaupe'; and after that, in crowded succession, 120 others."

All the month which follows, the hevehe ceaselessly dance and play their drums on the beach, accompanied by bands of dancing women for whom this is a period of gaiety and pride. At the end of this time, the masks vanish into the eravo in ceremonial procession. Later they are ritually shot to death with arrows—the women lamenting passionately meanwhile—after which the masks are secretly dismantled and burned, away in the bush. In the closing episodes, three bush pigs must be hunted and killed. The final rite of the cycle is a man hunt followed by a purification ceremony in which three plaited coco leaf images are thrown about the eravo, then tossed to the crowd outside to be trampled underfoot. They are called Iko: after the great hero who is also known is Hido in the western Gulf, and Sido in Kiwai.

39 Semese mask at Kerema, Spring 1912

8 MATERIALS, ARTISTS, AND FORMS

Materials and artists

The materials available to the Gulf artists are extremely limited, the most important being wood, cane, and bark. They chose—with deliberation, we may attempt to show—to limit themselves even more than is strictly necessary. Wood sculpture is confined to the ancestral boards, to drums, bull-roarers, a few figures, and small objects. The masks are essentially scaffoldings of cane, sometimes covered with decorated bark cloth. Apart from these major objects, the small personal and utilitarian articles are made of wood, bark, and coconut shell: belts, charms, spoons, combs, headrests and stools. Feathers are used for trimming hair ornaments and are also an important elaborating element of the masks. Structurally speaking all these objects are extremely simple; even the masks do not compare for sheer lavishness of material with the gorgeous synthetic constructions of the Sepik River tribes or the Marind-anim.

Carving tools are limited among the Namau (and probably throughout the area) to stone adzes and axes for rough work, and shell scrapers for finishing. Bone needles are used in sewing bark cloth on the masks and for attaching the strips of cane which outline the designs. Paint is laid on with a frayed pandanus branch; it usually consists of lime for white, red ochre, and charcoal for black. Surfaces are often charred as another method of obtaining black. The Elema increase this range by trading for pink ochre, yellow clay, and a soapstone which produces a wide range of greys.

Generally speaking, among the Namau, any man is capable of at least attempting to decorate his own canoe or bark belt, but is likely to call in a recognized expert either to carry it through from start to finish or at least to add final touches. He will pay for this, probably with shell ornaments. It seems likely this procedure was followed for other utilitarian objects.

Regrettably little is recorded about the making of the ritual objects, or their prescribed makers. The construction of the large masks is a communal affair among the Namau, except for the very few named ones: these are made by the leaders of the ravi's "sides," or groups of larava. Among the Elema a hevehe mask is, formally speaking, made by its owner, with help from his maternal uncle or a friend, but others may join in under the owner's supervision. Kovave are in theory the work of the maternal uncles, but are often carried out by anyone interested. Besides, old and learned men are usually on hand to offer advice and criticism about the traditional designs. One may guess that the same applies to the making of other objects as well: that those intended for communal use are made communally, those for presentation to initiates (such as gope

a

boards) by maternal uncles. Elementary as these statements may seem, it is impossible to enlarge on this interesting matter.

A great proportion of the art of New Guinea is two-dimensional and symmetrical; it takes only the most cursory examination to see that this is true of most Papuan Gulf work. There are few exceptions of minor importance. The carving, being as a general rule either engraving or in the shallowest possible relief, can hardly be thought of as very different from the designs formed on the masks by cane outlines filled in with paint. Indeed it is not easy to define at what point Papuan Gulf art makes the transition between—in the European senses—painting and sculpture. Moreover it often seems closer to our idea of design than of art. One major achievement of Papuan Gulf art, indeed, lies in the brilliant invention it shows in design redeemed from the insignificance of pattern-making by the fact that it describes some of the most vigorous and startling formalizations of the human figure ever created.

Recurrent forms in the Papuan Gulf

In analyzing the art of a primitive culture, we can often trace a vocabulary of primary forms which recur through most of, or all, its works. According to the needs of the artist and the resources of his culture, they may be many or few. Even when the art styles of a particular tribal area are sufficiently distinct, such basic forms may extend far beyond it: this is especially true of some parts of Africa. The critic's first reaction will (very properly) be the assumption that this is a case of one group's having invented these traits, after which others have taken them up. The process is covered by the word "influence"—which in Papuan societies may also encompass both trade and theft. However, "influence" implies historical sequences of which we generally know nothing. The very broad records of migration in the Gulf are not detailed enough for elaborate discussion, though they may prove suggestive. We should probably be wiser to think of change rather than development when Papuan Gulf art is concerned, and of rather rapid change at that. The recurrence of a certain specific type of object in separate areas need not necessarily imply "influence"; when such an object is statistically rare, this may rather suggest the historical increase or decrease of that object's popularity in an area: a process familiar enough to us by the name of "fashion." We must in most cases be content with the idea that a fundamental vocabulary of forms can be common to a large area, comprising a number of peoples, within which the artists of smaller areas compose with the vocabulary each in his own or his local style.

Unfortunately for the critic's pride in his ingenuity, the range of such forms in the Gulf area is unusually small. They are simple, geometric, and combined into works of a not very complex order. The most elaborate combination is never more than a single three-dimensional form with a surface dressing of two-dimensional forms—and it is the profusion of these which may give the total work an (often deceptive) appearance of great complexity. On the other hand, we should not be misled by the simplicity of the fundamental forms into underrating the importance of their roles in Gulf art.

There are both two- and three-dimensional forms of this nature. The most common two-dimensional surface is in the form of a long, flat oval: this applies to the ancestral boards, whatever their local names, from all the groups which have been described. It constitutes the form of the most spectacular type of masks found throughout the area; and is also, of course, the shape of those most sacred of all objects, the bull-roarers.

The two-dimensional vocabulary of detailing is dominated in the central area and the east by two main features: rows of small triangles and chevrons; and flowing, calligraphic lines enclosing blank spaces; in the west by set conventions for features and, again, small geometrical elements. Of the possible three-dimensional forms, the cone is the basis of several other types of mask. In effect, the kaiaimunu animals are similarly horizontal cones supported on legs (in former times they had

b   c   d, e

none). One might add that the Namau ravi and Elema eravo building is virtually a bisected cone laid with the curved side up, and that the outline of its entrance end is also that of the upper part of a kwoi. It may be mentioned that to the eastern Elema at least the eravo's façade recalls the face of a warrior; and, of course, the kwoi's main decoration is a human face. The ravi entrance and the gaping mouths of the kaiaimunu are also reminiscent of the jaws of drums through the whole area. These shapes are all so much the products of artifice (rather than derived from nature) that we may well doubt whether they represent a mode of seeing, but need not hesitate over their expressing a preference for things to be seen.

We may also take it they represent chosen methods of making. On the physical level, it is plain enough that the frameworks of a kaiaimunu animal, and a conical mask, and a ravi can be, and in practice are, almost identical in construction (see Williams, 1923, 1924). There was no reason why other methods should not have been used, and other works produced. In the case of masks, for instance, the Gulf people had no reason not to carve wooden ones, as was done in Kiwai and among the Gogodara—indeed, a tradition of the Elema states that they did use wood masks until a hero discovered the present style. Granted, however, the shapes they wished to use and the desire for monstrous size: their techniques of manufacture and the forms themselves could hardly be better suited to each other. The third item—the material—suited manufacture and form as ideally: hence the Gulf people's use of it.

We may also become aware of the interplay between the favored shapes and their mythological appropriateness. Thus if the kaiaimunu animal resembles a ravi, we recall that the kaiaimunu was, in legend, man's first habitation. Various hints that the ancestral boards and large oval masks have some reference to the bull-roarer have already been retailed. However, at this point we touch the domains of symbolism and significance, which may be more properly examined separately.

40 a Bull-roarer. Purari Delta: Namau. Wood, white paint, total length 36". Museum of Primitive Art 59.140. b, c Entrances of ravis at Kaimari, 1924. d Kaiaimunu animal in an Era River men's house, 1930. e Drum. Purari Delta: Namau. Chicago 10303

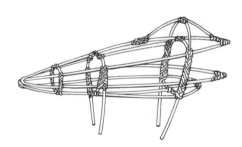

41 Top to bottom, frameworks of a kaiaimunu animal (after Williams, 1923); a mask; a Namau ravi (after Williams, 1924)

9 EMOTION AND SIGNIFICANCE

42 *Namau ancestral board* (kwoi). *Maipua. Wood, paint, 36½" high. Chicago 142393. 43 Elema ancestral board* (hohao) *in ceremonial house at Vailala, Spring 1912*

One of the most fascinating questions posed by a work from an alien culture is how we are to see it, for a work of art is not only itself. We, at this time and place, are habituated to the idea that a painting or a sculpture is potent to the extent that it is an independent being, speaking to us with its own voice. This is an attitude that creates a ready sympathy for primitive art, an open receptiveness. It may, however, be a fallacious sympathy.

In the whole range of primitive art, there are probably no works more overtly aggressive than some of the Elema ancestral tablets, none better suited to justify the equation of "primitive" with "savage." This is undoubtedly due to the staring eyes, the wide ferocious mouths, the rows of saw-tooth designs: all seem evidences of a deliberate striving for the terrific. Now the society which created these carvings was a gathering of men who by our standards were exceptionally violent and aggressive, and who indeed were expected to display these qualities to be accepted as admirable or even effectual. We in turn would expect their works to reflect their ways, and so in fact, we may agree, these tablets do.

But to what extent does this correspondence really exist? In practice the Elema are, by the standards of the Gulf, a relatively mild group. They are not cannibals, they profess a fairly strict morality, their religious practices have an atmosphere of good humor. They are fearful and disgusted by the western natives who eat men, prostitute their wives and terrorize their initiates—"Kiwai fashion" is the opprobrious phrase for reprehensible, unpleasant actions. Yet the Namau kwoi, for instance, may appear much less alarmist than the Elema hohao, involving as they do flowing lines and graceful curves. In terms of the Gulf, then, we may look alternatively upon this Elema "ferocity" as fraudulent; as an expression of what they would like to be; or as an effect of our own self-deception.

Every work of art, whatever its own qualities, is also the focus of a congeries of associations which at many times and in many places have blinded the viewer to the inherent qualities. We should obviously guard against falling into this trap where primitive art is concerned. A first temptation is to consider it all as high art. I say temptation because this may lead us to an over-portentous, over-flattering view of any particular object. It is rather creditable to ourselves to think of all these things as having high seriousness; as being exotic, terrifying and "religious." We forget that these appurtenances of his daily life cannot be exotic to a Papuan; that through daily habit a great deal of the terror surrounding many of the most ferocious appearing objects must eventually wear off; that his conception of religion may be very different from ours. We may nevertheless try to assess something of the associations which cluster, for a Gulf man, around his art.

The extremely violent emotional associations of the objects in some of the cultures must almost inevitably escape us. Few sane members of our society are capable of a full imaginative participation in the circumstances of initiation in which the objects are sometimes first seen; accompanied as initiations are in some areas, for the girls by legitimized rape, and for boys and girls alike by such fright that the initiatory enclosure becomes "like a cesspool." (Riley, 1925 : 39.)

Again, we can hardly imagine the low degree of man-made stimulation to the visual sense among these people. It was less than could be found in other areas of New Guinea (where so often almost every household object was brilliantly decorated), and infinitely lower than it is among ourselves. To the young boy or girl entering a ceremonial house for the first time, or to the women on their rare visits, in the west; or during the appearances of the masks in the east; the aesthetic experience must have been almost overwhelmingly rich, and the sense of human accomplishment conveyed by these objects far greater than it can be to us. We can guess, if we cannot participate in, the impact of these sights on people whose day-to-day experience of aesthetically shaped objects did not go much beyond the carving on a stool or a club. Without exaggerating, we should probably remember that the first revelation of art to the Papuan Gulf man or woman was usually an emotionally and physically tumultuous one which was renewed occasionally for the women, and gradually wore off for the men as they became habituated to adult life.

The question of sacredness involves attitudes to religion which are partly foreign to us, partly familiar. Certain objects are certainly more sacred, or powerful or awe-inspiring to the Gulf man than are others; but we cannot relate these differences to the art motives. Some hohao and some kwoi are more important in this sense than others, but there is nothing to indicate that this bears any relation to the actual designs carved on them; nor is any design, or any variety of designs, associated with sanctity. The gope of the Kerewa are apparently another case; somewhat contradictory statements by Austen (1934) and Wirz (1937) imply that differences in size and depth of carving are associated with the different grades of importance. However, it can be shown from actual examples that exactly the same conventions may be used on very large and very small gope; so here again the kind of design is neither associated with nor dictates the degree to which the object is valued. Again, it is worth taking an instance in which the choice of material and decoration reaches its highest degree of subjectivity in this area. To our eyes there can surely be very little difference between the kind of branch or fragment recognized as an imunu, or made into a kakame, and one selected for a utilitarian stool. Furthermore, although it may be significant that the designs on a kwoi may also be used on a bull-roarer—and this we appreciate because it seems to have a basis in religious logic—it is perhaps equally significant that the same designs may appear on a stool and a kakame.

We can hardly fall back with any confidence on the idea that the designs are at all hallowed by long tradition or great antiquity. Meagre as the evidence is, it seems likely that the Papuan Gulf was settled by its present population fairly recently. It is certainly true that the adoption or the development of certain cults took place almost within living memory. We may expect that the elaboration of the art styles connected with them took place simultaneously, though of course we cannot guess anything about the antecedents of the particular designs involved.

If we are to consider the makers' attitude, we must realize that for them objects were made awe-inspiring by their associations. The relative age of the objects was of prime importance: hohao, kwoi and Purari Delta masks became more loaded with power the older they became. Agiba took on power with the addition of paint (and, no doubt, of skulls). The *kind* of power is not familiar to us: it is "heat," menace, danger. The magic of the imunu was projected on to these things and seemed to radiate inexplicably from them. This, on the other hand, is familiar to us, as a fragment of the True Cross is judged holier than the ceiling of the Sistine Chapel.

Another important conception is also less familiar: the idea of the work of art, or the religious object, operating as a social force. The details of the makers' relations to each other are not so much involved here as the relation of the object to the culture. The agiba are a case in point. As they represent ancestral males and females, the attachment of the skulls to their vertical uprights clearly represents an assimilation of the dead to the clan.

It may be hazarded that "gope," in their various forms, also represent some concept of assimilation. Thus, the gope of Urama-Wapo, and their counterparts the Namau kwoi, are placed in close contact with skulls. At Kaimari the kaiaimunu animals are called gopiravi (= gope-men's house), and the bodies pushed into them are pulled out through a hole in the stomach. It is tempting to see this as a symbol of the victim's being reborn as a member of the larava which owns the kaiaimunu, just as its boys are carried in the kaiaimunu's mouth. Finally, at Maipua the spirits of the raid victims are, specifically, "gope." Yet another kind of symbolic assimilation to the group takes place among the Gogodara, where the boys are placed at initiation in model canoes (gi), ornamented with totemic designs. These, according to Wirz (1937) represent the totem animals which swallow the initiates and give them new life with tribal status.

Such conceptions are to some extent actually reflected by the treatment and subjects of the works of art. The main subject of all Papuan Gulf art is the human figure. Animals are rare in the western Gulf apart from those images used for ceremonial purposes or used as headrests. In the east they are common on the Elema eharo masks. Plants seem to be figured occasionally in the east, again on eharo and on Orokolo hevehe masks, but apparently do not appear at all in the west. As one would expect in these head-hunting cultures, the main focus is on the human head. Apart from the small figures of the Wapo-Era district (agiba and bioma), and a few larger ones from the Namau and Elema, the trunk and limbs are minimized to the conventional patterns or mere lines seen on the Kerewa gope; or apparently disappear, as on the Namau kwoi. The hands and arms of the figures on such boards (and often the freestanding figures) are upraised in a gesture certainly used by women in dancing (Williams, 1940: pl. 11, 51, 52), but here possibly protective. The Kerewa reception of Europeans has been mentioned. To take an example from another Papuan culture, Kooijman (1960) describes the Asmat encountering Europeans "raising their arms and stretching out their hands . . . to protect themselves . . . from . . . unknown dangers. . . . The gesture was accompanied by cries of 'Papisj, papisj' [a protective ceremonial wife-exchange rite]"; and he comments that this gesture appears to be shown on the Asmat war shields.

Though often abridged, the full human figure seems always implied. Even the typical Namau kwoi, with its central face surrounded by four bands of chevrons, perhaps vaguely alludes to a full figure after all; the torsos on Turama gope are formed by such bands. On many Namau and Elema boards appears a dot-in-circle design, often connected to the mouth by a vertical line; Haddon describes this as a shell ornament (1894), but like the four-pointed star of the Kerewa agiba, it certainly represents a navel. This apparently curious stress is perhaps quite reasonable, as the Elema describe a lineage as hekore haruapo: "one navel" (and the word larave means "navel-cord"). The torso and limbs sometimes take on ambiguous forms: thus they will appear as a crocodile or lizard form, the tail of which can be construed as a penis.

The designs on Wapo-Era gope (and their related neighbors) are similarly stylizations of the hocker figure as it is explicitly engraved on one tobacco pipe, and silhouetted in the bioma and agiba figures. On one gope indeed there occur at least two such figures with raised arms, one above the other. The typical fragmented elements at the sides are clearly related to the stylized figures placed down the length of the bull-roarer, but divided vertically to form designs which also recur as gunwale patterns on canoes. In this context, they are de-

44 Tobacco pipe (detail). Era River delta. Coll. P. Wirz, 1930. Bamboo. Basel Vb 7780. 45 Bull-roarer (kaiaimunu) (detail). Era River. Coll. P. Wirz, 1930. Wood, paint, total length 25½". Amsterdam 2670–293

44, 45

scribed as kewekemuri—a word obviously related to "keweke" as a name for the large masks. The large oval keweke (or aiaimunu) masks of this area are decorated on each side of the midrib with a single long form flowing upward from the lower part of the face, and connected with or surrounding the vision ports. The forked ends of these show clearly that they represent upraised arms and hands.

Among the individual features, the looped faces of the Kerewa masks perhaps represent not so much exaggerated noses as the boards decorating the trophy skulls; or, if not a representation, are an equivalent.

The forehead and brows figure so prominently, perhaps, because the brow is the foremost part of the body when a man rushes at an enemy: so in Kiwai it symbolizes fighting (Landtman, 1927: 151). The further connection of brows and war is shown by the "thundercloud" pad worn by kaiaimunu animals and war leaders among the Namau.

A most striking aspect of many Gulf carvings is the prominence given to the eye. We cannot plumb the psychological reasons for the negation of the body, but possibly the stress on the eyes is explained by Landtman's statements (1927: 11, 13, 325) that among the Kiwai bloodshot eyes are the sign of the great warrior or sorcerer, that enemies' eyes are kept for war magic, and that eyebrows buried under darimo posts help the men find victims in war—"spy them out" in fact. We have seen that the Kerewa gope are not only protective but involved in war magic, and by analogy perhaps they too are intended to look for enemies. Such was no doubt also the reason for the eye designs carved on the western and Purari Delta war canoes: but here a social aspect enters. In the western Gulf areas of Wapo, Era, Urama, and in the Purari Delta, the flowing eye designs carved on the canoes are the local type of clan insignia. A canoe, jointly owned by members of a clan, was a visible expression of their solidarity (hence the Gogodara question of a stranger, "What is your canoe?"). Clan insignia and ownership designs are indeed common throughout the area. The Gogodara mask panels carry totemic clan designs (tao), as do the smaller plaques (ikewa) sometimes attached to the conical diba headdress. The tao are also employed as ownership marks on trees. How far the western Gulf canoe designs corresponded to actual face painting is not clear; few of the Namau face designs, Williams figures (1924), seem relevant; however a Purari over-modelled skull of uncertain provenience has painted designs which are very similar to specific canoe designs. In spite of the consistencies mentioned earlier for Urama, field photographs show that in the long houses of Wapo, Era, and the Purari Delta, in which at least one design usually recurs, considerable latitude may be found in the gope or kwoi of a single cubicle. Thus it is difficult to determine the degree of social consistency applied in the use of these designs on the ancestral boards: whether the variety is due to personal taste or whether it is based on a social factor, such as marriage.

These eye designs are the main feature of the important keweke masks (Urama), aiaimunu masks (Purari Delta) and semese masks (eastern Elema): as becomes clear if we visualize a number of them arranged up a vertical axis. The masks thus represent a reiterated, and so additionally strengthened, statement of ancestral unity. At the same time, they must have been at once belligerent and protective—like the gope and kwoi they resemble in form. The close relationship of masks and boards is further exemplified by a type of Era River mask with a face surmounting the main face, found repeated exactly in bioma figures and a type of Namau kwoi.

This, of course, applies only to those masks with rigidly symmetrical designs. In the Purari Delta, these appear to be found mainly among the coastal Namau, with their strong ancestral affiliations with the west. The asymmetric designs of the inland Namau masks are of great beauty in their freedom. It may well be, however, that it was an eccentric freedom; the Koriki Namau at least profess ignorance about the meaning of such designs, and perhaps they are merely misunderstandings of the eye design complex.

The relationship among bull-roarers, ancestral boards, and masks has been canvassed in considerable detail by Williams and Wirz, although Williams (1939) insists on the fundamental independence of the cults in practice and in native thought. But it seems indisputable that the three form a constellation of objects, even if their connection in their owners' minds is largely unconscious. To this group we may add the canoes in their assimilative or collective aspect. We have seen that Kiwai gope are actually canoe ornaments, and that the Kerewa gope, the kwoi and the hohao are made from old canoes; that some kwoi are bordered with canoe gunwale designs. So are the Wapo-Era bull-roarers, and also some of the aiaimunu masks.* It may not be too much to suggest that, however obliquely, these ritual objects have reference to, if not actual identity with, the communal canoes.

Still another possible grouping of the ritual objects shows an emotional dynamism. One may guess that in the Papuan Gulf there is a tension between the desire to have a secret and the desire to display the secret. The initiated men must conceal much of their ritual life from the women and uninitiated boys: but to do so completely would be to starve their need to assert their sexual superiority. That they are not altogether easy about this assertion is disclosed by the Namau legend that women actually first discovered masks and bull-roarers. But, if we take a rather all-inclusive view of the Gulf cultures, we can build up the following imaginative sequence:

1 The most sacred objects, the thunder-voiced kaiaimunu, are kept in association with the thunder-noise producing bull-roarers, all in strict secrecy.

2 Bull-roarer-shaped boards (kaiaimunu) are kept in secrecy, but versions of these are placed where they can be seen by any man, whether initiated to the bull-roarer cult or not.

3 Unimportant versions of gope are given to young uninitiated boys who have not yet seen the men's gope.

4 Bull-roarer- and gope-shaped masks are worn publicly, so that some version of their form is revealed even to the women who will never see the objects they really represent.

Thus the same form is repeated in, so to speak, wider and wider contexts of decreasing secrecy. By the time the aiaimunu mask reaches the audience of women its prototype, the bull-roarer, is already at several removes. Its "heat" is safely dissipated. The secret is safe, yet has been revealed far enough to prevent its retention from being a source of frustration rather than satisfaction.

* The "behavior" of the objects is also comparable: the Kerewa gope (kaiaimunu) move as war omens, the kaiaimunu animals rock the war canoes.

46 Gogodara tao designs: left to right, iobo, boinare, tao-sibara, ägia. From P. Wirz, 1934a

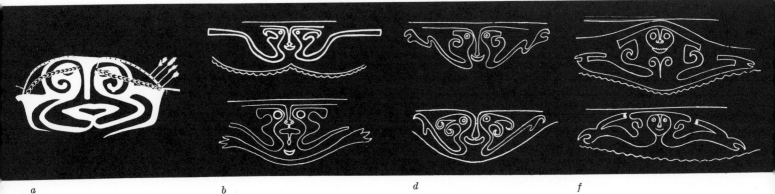

a   b   d   f
     c   e   g

47a Face-paint designs on a Purari Delta over-modelled skull, British Museum 1944. Oc 2. 1939. b–g Canoe prow clan designs from b, Purari Delta; c–e, g, Era River; f, Wapo. From P. Wirz, 1934

	KIWAI	BAMU R	TURAMA R	KEREWA	URAMA I	WAPO CR	ERA R	INLAND NAMAU	COASTAL NAMAU	WESTERN ELEMA	CENTRAL ELEMA	EASTE... ELEM...
men's house: one entrance	darimo	dubu daimo	darimo	dubu daima	daimo	daimo						
two entrances								weneh	r a v i		e r a v o	
mask: round head long nose		k a u	v a	i								
round head loop nose			kavai	kavai /avoko								
round head open jaws								kanipu	kanipu/avoko			
conical										eharo	kovave	harisu	oioi
conical with emblems									abo-abo	eharo		
small oval									kanipu			
large oval							k e w e k e	a i a i m u n u		hevehe	s e m e s e
ancestral boards	gope		gope/kaiaimunu		g o p e			k w o i		hohao/kaiavuru	
bull-roarers	madubu/gope						k a i a i m u n u	u p u r a		kaiavuru		tiparu
skull-holders		tutuapu	a g i b a									
small skull-holders		gope		na-agiba marabu								
flat figures						agiba/bioma		kwoi				
figures in round	mimia			agiba		kakame				hohao		
decorated natural objects		imunu				i m u n u						
paired figures				l r i v a k e			lgovake				semes...
animal figures						k a i a i m u n u					

Chart: the distribution of types and names of objects in the Papuan Gulf area. Shaded areas indicate probability of occurrence

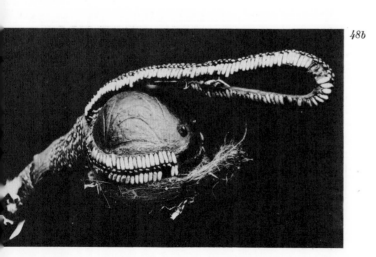

48b

GOGODARA   The Gogodara tribe live in the swamp and grass plain country around the Aramia River, the Bamu's largest affluent. A somewhat isolated group, their culture is similar in many respects to those of their neighbors, but has a number of striking variations. They lay great stress on totemic organization, and their totemic designs (tao) have already been mentioned. These are mostly based on concentric circles with asymmetric additions: they figure prominently on all ceremonial objects, and are even painted on the bodies of those taking part in rites.

The tao are thus basic motifs of Gogodara art. The near-mathematical regularity of the circular forms, and on the other hand the asymmetry of the total designs, moreover constitute the art's fundamental character and its departure from the other styles of the Gulf. The other conventions of Gogodara art—the round human heads, crescentic boar tusks and crocodile teeth—are stated with a much more repetitive exactitude than they would be anywhere else.

Most Gogodara work—except the king posts of the long houses, the ladders and drums—is carried out in a light pith

36

wood. Two features about their decoration are distinctive: the designs are painted on rather than carved or engraved; the colors are not limited to the usual austere range of red, white, and black, but also include browns and yellow ochres. These, combined with the wood's natural buff, give a very wide range of color, enhanced by a use of red seeds and discs of mother-of-pearl. A further enrichment is provided by feathers, sometimes cut and twisted into elaborate trophies. All in all, Gogodara art is the gayest and most decorative of the Papuan Gulf—with all the limitations on inventiveness or vigor those adjectives imply.

Its antecedents or relationships are hard to define. The ornamental plaques (ikewa) fastened to the conical diba head-dresses seem such schematic versions of the large masks found farther east that one is tempted to speculate whether the Gogodara actually invented this mode. However, a closer approach to the decorativeness of their productions is to be found away from the Gulf area, in the trophy heads and ceremonial rattles of the upper Fly River.

48a Figure, tao design sibara. Light wood, paint, mother of pearl, cowrie shell, abrus seeds, about 48" high. Collection Mr. and Mme Henri Kramer. 48b Rattle in form of imitation trophy head. Upper Fly River. Coconut, cane, seeds

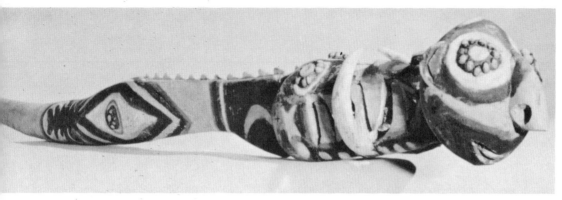

49

50

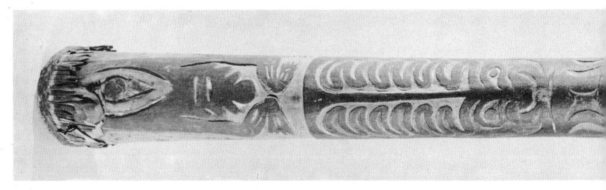

51, 52, 53

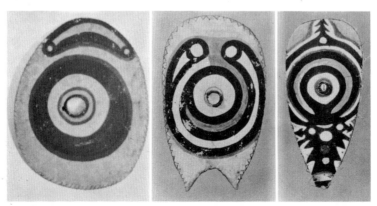

54 55 56

GOGODARA

49 Model of a ceremonial canoe (gi), tao design si-bara. Aketa. Coll. P. Wirz, 1930. Light wood, paint, abrus seeds, mirror fragment, 45⅝" long; original length about 156". MPA 60.92. 50 Drum. Wood, black and white paint, cane, hide, 68⅛" long. MPA 59.264. 51 Ceremonial head ornament (ikewa), tao design boinare. Coll. A. B. Lewis, 1912. Light wood; red seeds; shell; rattan binding; black, brown, yellow ochre on buff paint; 18½" in diameter. Chicago 142764. 52 Ceremonial head ornament (ikewa), tao design ägia. Coll. P. Wirz, 1930. Light wood; rattan; cord; mussel shell; abrus seeds; white, red and black paint; 17¾" high. Amsterdam 2670–382. 53 Ceremonial head ornament (ikewa), tao design sibara. Coll. P. Wirz, 1930. Light wood, heron feathers, cyprea snail shell, abrus seeds, paint, 17" high. Amsterdam 2670–383. 54 Mask, tao design iobo. Coll. A. B. Lewis, 1912. Light wood; red seeds; rattan border binding; black, brown, white on buff paint; 30⅝" high. Chicago 142766. 55 Mask. Kubu. Coll. A. C. Haddon, 1914. Light wood; red seeds; feathers; black, red, yellow and white paint; 40" high. Cambridge 16.143.293. 56 Mask. Light wood; earth red, black and white paint; feathers, 28¼" high. Chicago 142770. 57 Figure. Light wood, shell, paint, 48½" high. Oxford

58

59   60

KIWAI AREA

The historical fact of the western Gulf's having been popu-
lated both by indigenous tribes and by immigrants from Kiwai
has already been stated. Granted the vigor of the newcomers'
culture, a strong influence by the Kiwai styles on the art styles
of the area is only to be expected. Naturally a large number of
art styles can be distinguished in the huge Kiwai area—from
Torres Strait to the east bank of the Fly River—but not all of
their characteristics, by any means, need to be taken into account.

A first consideration must be the connections between Torres Strait art and that of Kiwai. The facial convention used
in the Saibai Island masks (whether wooden or tortoise shell)
consists of an elongated inverted triangular face with horizontal brows, a small, grinning mouth with bared teeth and—
most prominent of all—a huge nose with a long bridge, wide
nostrils and sharply turned-in septum. This becomes modified
in the smaller Kiwai carvings (such as the heads on digging
sticks) into drop-shaped heads, truncated at the top, with the
same facial features. The decorative adjuncts to the turtle
shell masks—strips of turtle shell carved in openwork patterns
—are also relevant: parallel bars connected by diagonals so op-
posed as to form bisected diamonds.

The bodies of the small mimia pendants are usually covered
with a design of the same geometric order which recurs so
often it must be defined: a circle or diamond flanked on either

58 Dugong hunting charm? Torres Strait or lower Fly River. Wood, 24" long. Collection Mr..Allan Frumkin. 59 Mask. Torres Strait. Wood, red, black, white paint, 28⅜" high. Royal Scottish Museum, Edinburgh 1885.81. 60 Staff used in Moguru ceremony. Bamu River, Aropai. Coll. A. B. Lewis, 1912. Wood, 20⅞" long. Chicago 142740. 61 Pendant figure (mimia). Lower Fly River. Wood, 12⅞" high. Pitt-Rivers Museum, Burrows coll., Oxford. 62 Pendant figure

(mimia). Lower Fly River. Wood, white paint, fibre, cloth, 13¼" long. Wellcome Historical Medical Museum 23.1952. 63 Canoe board (gope). Fly River, Tirio. Wood, paint, 40" high. Chicago 142877. 64 Canoe board (gope). Lower Fly River. Wood, paint. Baltimore Museum of Art, Wurtzburger coll. 55.251.93. 65 Canoe board (gope). Lower Fly River. Wood, paint, feathers, 23" long. Rijksmuseum voor Volkenkunde, Leiden 2403-N:28

side by bands of parallel chevrons. It seems possible that this design is based on a commonly-worn ornamental band of coix lachryma seeds on a woven strip (Haddon 1901–35, 4, pl. ix, 1) from the Torres Strait.

The faces of these pendants are in a relief convention which is of paramount importance in western Gulf art, and it occurs in many variations. At its most elaborate in Kiwai—and in other places it is often a good deal less than elaborate—it consists of a brow with a widow's peak elongated into the bridge of the nose, at the lower end of which is an outlined V representing the mouth. The eyes consist of concentric circles. From the tip of the brow form, on each side, depends a rounded lappet which turns inward under the mouth. Serrations on the top of the brow, or on a border above it, here and elsewhere probably represent the cassowary feather circlet worn by men.

At its best, this convention is highly successful in its clear definition of a field and the features within it.

At the opposite extreme is the extraordinarily relaxed version of it employed on the handsome canoe gope of the Fly estuary's banks—a version almost entirely dependent for its coherence on the shape of the board, and the symmetrical balancing of the eyes with circles on the cheeks. The design is exceptional in this reliance on extraneous factors: most Gulf designs either dominate their field or show a fine disregard for its exigencies. Nevertheless, the boards have an eerie vitality of their own.

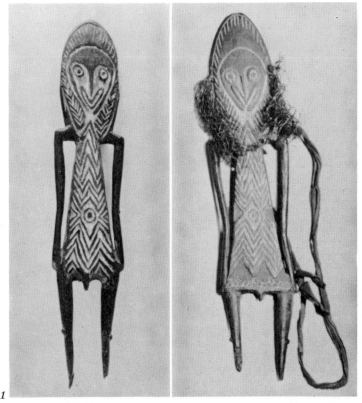

66   67   68   69

LOWER FLY RIVER

A remarkable group of human figures in the round, about half life-size, is associated with the provenience "Girara, between the Fly and Bamu Rivers," and are said to have been made for the Moguru. "Girara" was formerly employed as a tribal name for the Gogodara, with whose art style these figures have nothing in common. They are related, rather, to the art styles of Kiwai, and may therefore be ascribed to the north bank of the Fly. Some of the large ones are apparently paired, male and female, and these share definite stylistic features. A number of smaller figures in the same styles suggests that the whole group may equally be mimia figures and their "children."

These magnificent figures are the most fully conceived sculptures from the Gulf area, and certainly the most naturalistic. This however should not obscure the fact that in a couple of cases the heads embody unmistakably the conventions of the Saibai masks. On the other hand the undercut breasts and the legs suggest a relationship to the style of the Binaturi River in the west, as does another type of face with squared-off jaws. This might well also be a local variant of the Kiwai-style heads found on paddles and digging sticks.

One extraordinary drum from the same district seems (though sexed as male) to illustrate a legend about the origin of the Dibiri (Bamu River) drums: the beheaded body of a girl became hard, like wood, and flies hollowed it out so that it only needed a tympanum over the neck to be completed.

42

70   71   72   76

73   74

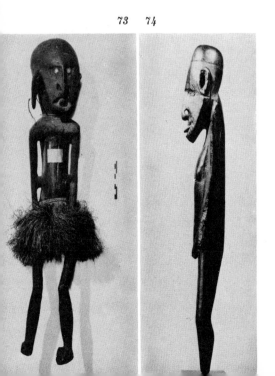

75

66–72 Figures used for Moguru ceremony. Chicago examples coll. E. Baxter Riley, acquired A. B. Lewis, 1912. Wood. 66 British Museum. 67 40¾" high. Chicago 142783.
68 Pearl shell eyes, 37" high. Chicago 142784. 69 36" high. Chicago 142785. 70 40⅞"
high. Chicago 142782. 71 43⅝" high. Chicago 142781. 72 Coll. E. Baxter Riley. 36"
high. Collection Mr. and Mrs. Raymond Wielgus. 73 Figure used for Moguru ceremony?
Raffia skirt; 25½" high. Cambridge 04.366. 74 Figure used for Moguru ceremony?
Traces of red paint, 12⅝" high. Collection Mr. and Mrs. Raymond Wielgus. 75 Head
used for Moguru ceremony. Chicago 142789. 76 Drum. 36" high. Chicago 142777

77, 78, 79

80

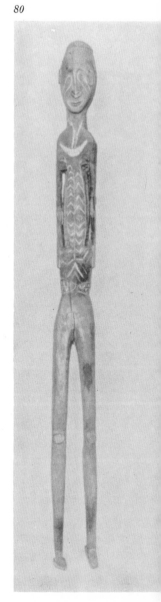

81

77–79 Clubs. Bamu River Delta. Coll. P. Wirz, 1930. 77 Palm wood,
traces red paint, 46½" long. Amsterdam 2670–351. 78 Hardwood,
traces red paint, 50¾" long. Amsterdam 2670–358. 79 Wood; red,
black and white paint; 50" long. Amsterdam 2670–352. 80–82 Figures for use in Moguru ceremony. Coll. P. Wirz, 1930. 80 Woman.
Wood, paint. Basel Vb 8066. 81 Woman. Buniki. Wood, red and blue
paint, 100" high. Collection Mr. Serge Brignoni. 82 Animals: a, pig;
b, pig; c, bird; d, crocodile. Baniro, Buniki or Opati. Soft wood, 17⅜",
20", 17⅜", 74⅞" long. After Wirz, 1934: Taf. XI, 1, 2, 3, 4.

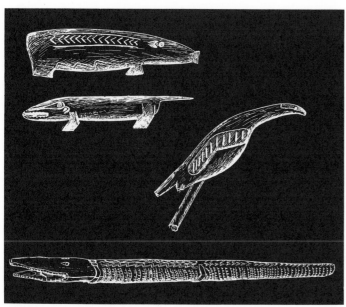

82

Few objects are extant from the Bamu River; nor, perhaps,
given the low population of this infertile area, should we
expect there to be many. Most apparently stem from the delta
and these, as one might expect, show the effect of the cultural
pressures from east and west to such a degree that we can
hardly speak of there being any genuine Bamu style at all.

Many objects show a close consistency with Kiwai traits—
probably in direct ratio to the contacts of their original owners
with the home island. Clubs are decorated, in a stiffly un-
imaginative manner characteristic of Kiwai, with registers of
zigzags between parallel lines; the same zigzags occur on the
nose boards of the decorated trophy skulls. They also ornament
sculptures of men and animals displayed in the Moguru ceremonies. Some of these are on an ambitious scale which gives
them a clumsy impressiveness; but their rigidity is that of the
poorer type of Kiwai figure sculpture.

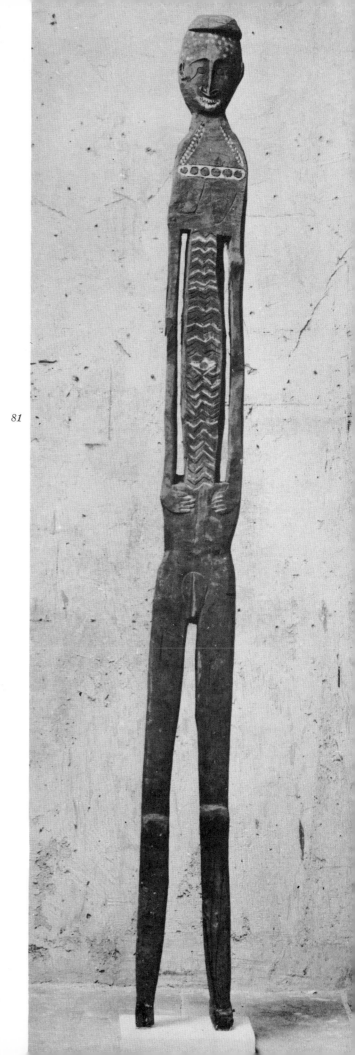

83

84

85

86

87

BAMU RIVER

One small agiba from the Bamu Delta shows both the outline and the characteristic face design of a Fly River canoe gope; indeed one such gope is attributed to the Bamu, and may actually be a local product rather than an import. Another has a distinctly Kerewa figure on what is probably a Bamu field: that is, one in which the hooks are proportionately smaller and more vertical than is usual in Kerewa. The name for these boards in the Bamu region—tutuapu—apparently applies generally to the commonest design for a human face. This again seems to be, rather than the canoe gope design, the design which figures on the mimia pendants; and this will recur often in the area to the east. On the Bamu it is found, perhaps chiefly, on the lesser objects: tobacco tubes, paddle handles, head-carriers, and weapons.

More distinctive at first sight are the area's fine drums. These have long or short "jaws" which, with a band just be-

83 *Canoe board (gope). Wood, black, white, green paint. British Museum (F) [6]. 84 Agiba (tutuapu). Coll. P. Wirz, 1930: recent work. Wood, black and white paint; bird and animal skulls; 14⅛" high. Basel 7864. 85 Agiba (tutuapu). Coll. P. Wirz, 1930: recent work. Wood, white and red paint, 41⅜" high. After Wirz 1934; Taf. VIII, 2. 86 Agiba (gope). Dibiri Island, Wododo. Coll. A. C. Haddon, 1914. Wood, black, white, red paint; bird skulls; 20⅞" high. Cambridge. 87 Drum. Buniki. Coll. H.M.S. "Fly" expedition, 1845. Wood, red, black, white paint. British Museum 8833. 88 Mask (kauvai). Aropai. Coll. A. B. Lewis, 1912. Basketry, clay, raffia, red, white and black paint, about 30" high. Chicago 142732. 89 Mask (kauvai). Coll. A. B. Lewis, 1912. Basketry, clay, raffia, paint, 29⅛" high. Chicago 142729*

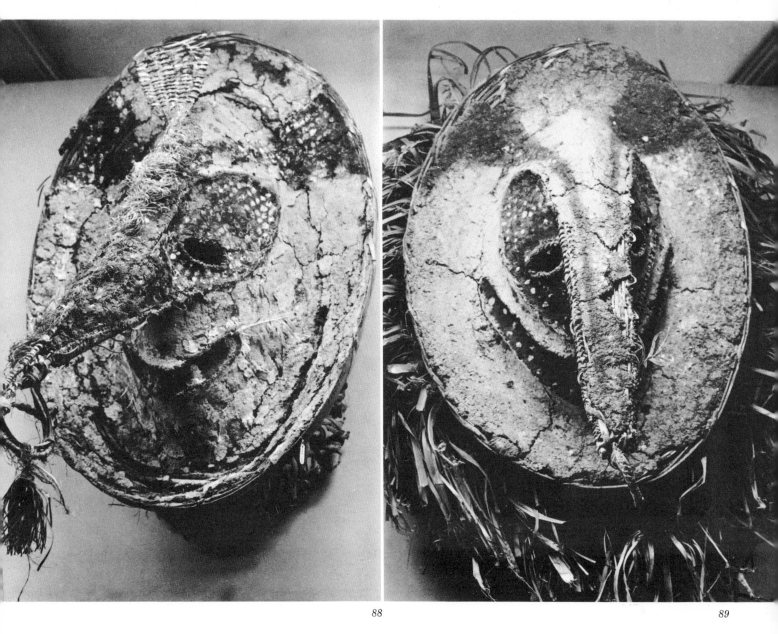

low them, are decorated with scroll-like designs boldly painted in red and white against the black which covers the rest of the drum. Made in Dibiri, these were certainly traded to Kiwai; one may suspect that they also went to Goaribari, or at least that the drums found there are close copies of Dibiri models. Taut and accomplished as they are, however, it is also possible to see the designs as symmetrically stylized versions of the tao (clan insignia) carved on Gogodara drums and tobacco pipes.

Perhaps the least influenced or derivative works from the Bamu are the kauvai masks, which apparently are made inland. These are distinguished by their long, straight noses tipped with small loops. Comparatively crudely made as they are, with their coating of clay over a plaited base, their finish —of white paint with quadrants of black, yellow, red spots, and a trim of yellow and white feathers—is curiously fresh and elegant.

Something of the same quality is shown in one type of trophy-skull decoration which is apparently also practised in the Kerewa district, though the best surviving examples ap-

pear to come from the Bamu. The skull is fitted with a wooden oval (Fly River: kaneka), originally garnished with yellow and white feathers, plugged into the nasal orifice; the face is covered with pearly grey coix lachryma seeds, as are the long pith plugs, tipped with red mucuna beans, inserted in the eye sockets. The gay colors make the skull not a terrifying image, like the upper Fly River stuffed heads, nor a noble one like those of the Sepik River, but one conveying the preciousness and high value these objects had for their collectors.

Trophy skulls. Torobina. S. D. Burrows coll., before 1914. Chicago 143965, 143964. 92 Trophy skull. 17½" long. British Museum (Beaseley coll. 1944 Oc 1939). 93 Trophy skull. Buniki. Coll. Judge Robinson, 1904. University of Aberdeen Anatomical Department

90

91

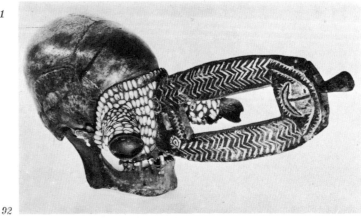

92

The ceremonial life of the Turamarubi is said to be rich; a contention borne out by their head-dance complex and their practice of the Moguru. However, a mere handful of Turama River pieces exist in our collections.

The rare basketry masks are summary in content, and merely blackened rather than decorated. While they are quite neatly made, their lack of elaboration seems to show an extraordinarily perfunctory attempt to create an image. This is particularly true of the examples with a nose in the form of a large loop. An example of the Bamu kauvai type, with a comparatively less elongated nose, also exists.

The gope share much of the same sketchy poverty of material and method. Some are old paddle blades, converted; all are carved in very low relief, with over-thin or over-thick blackened lines on (originally) white backgrounds. Nevertheless we are here, surprisingly enough, presented with the first genuinely local style since Kiwai. The coloration's very meagerness is distinctive. Even more so are the designs of figures in the hocker position, with torsos formed of four long ovals and with attenuated, straight limbs notched at the ends to indicate fingers and toes. By the Gulf's usual high standards these designs are naive; even so, a few examples show how elegant even this style could be in good hands.

94 Mask (avoko or kavai). Murigi Island. Coll. P. Wirz, 1930. Basketry, black paint, 36⅝" long. Basel Vb 7834. 95 Mask (avoko). Murigi Island. Coll. P. Wirz, 1930. Basketry, paint, 23⅝" long. Zürich 8544. 96 Canoe board? (gope). Coll. P. Wirz, 1930. Wood, black paint, feathers, 22⅜" high. Basel Vb 12548. 97 Gope. Coll. P. Wirz, 1930. Wood, black and white paint, 48⅞" high. Amsterdam 2670–275. 98 Gope. Coll. P. Wirz, 1930. Wood, 28⅜" high. Amsterdam 2670–277. 99 Gope. Coll. P. Wirz, 1930. Wood, black and white paint, 51⅛" high. Basel Vb 8026. 100 Gope. Coll. P. Wirz, 1930. Wood, black paint, 19⅝" high. Basel Vb 7816

96

99

100

98

97

51

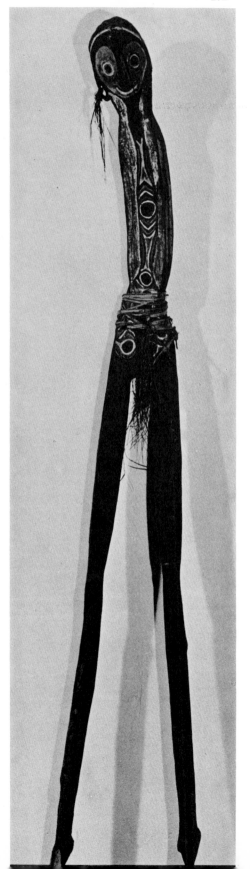

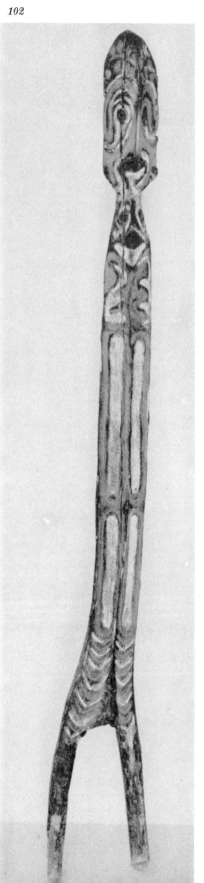

103

Some carvings follow completely in their essentials the manner of Kerewa area art; which is reasonable enough, as the Turamarubi of the delta have trade links with the Omati River. The large figures in particular share the qualities of the more spontaneous styles found in Kerewa.

*101 Figure for Moguru. Delta area.
Coll. P. Wirz, 1930. Hardwood, red
and white paint, 68" high. Amsterdam 2670–302. 102 Figure. Coll.
P. Wirz, 1930. Wood, paint, 68½"
high. Basel Vb 7862. 103 Door of
ceremonial house. Delta area. Coll.
P. Wirz, 1930. Wood, black and
white paint, 49⅛" high. Basel
7987. 104 Dance staff. Delta area.
Coll. P. Wirz, 1930. Wood, paint,
15¾" high. Basel Vb 7872*

105 Decorated skull. Coll. at Dopima 1901?
University of Aberdeen Anatomical Depart-
ment. 106 Mask (avoko). Basketry, paint,
feathers, raffia. Cambridge 29252. 107
Mask (avoko). Basketry, paint, raffia.
Chicago

KEREWA AREA

The Kerewa area has the most highly developed art styles of
the western Gulf. It also produces the greatest number of art
objects, and in general these show a much more accomplished
standard of craftsmanship than those from farther west. The
big basketry masks (avoko) are a case in point. Their plaiting
is finer and more regular, and their forms are both more confi-
dently stated and more substantial. As in the Turama examples, applied strips of cane outline curving forms on their
surfaces, but here these demarcate areas to be painted in red
and white. Unlike other Gulf works, resembling only each
other, they succeed brilliantly as images, bulky and sinister:
but to the extent that they are hardly susceptible to criticism.
They are triumphs of characterization, intentionally or not.

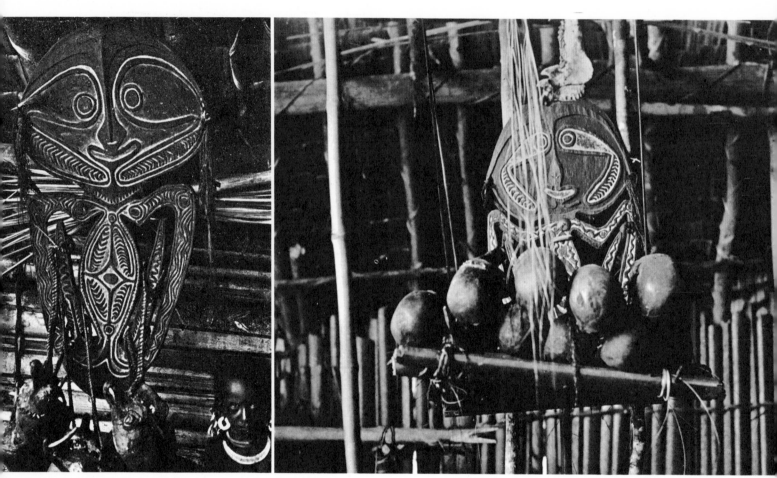

108   109

KEREWA AREA

A similar element of personality may be found in the agiba; it must have been stressed by the uncertain light of the men's houses where they were kept. Again, they are not quite like anything else; but they are of a much more complex form than the masks. Three examples of cross influence may be noticed. One, a Bamu agiba with a Kerewa figure, has been mentioned. Another small agiba from the Kerewa area has a scrolled face design exactly similar to that of an agiba from the Bamu estuary, besides its Bamu geometrical patterning and what has been described as the typical Bamu form. On the other hand,

still another agiba, though from the Kerewa district, presents an interesting possibility in its divergences from the more usual Kerewa styles. The designs on this large and old piece have distinct affinities with the somewhat straggling carving on Turama gope, which are all the more significant since no Turama agiba appears to be extant. The typical Kerewa agiba have proportionately huge, round heads, designed in the Kiwai mimia pendant facial convention. Here it is carried out with a superb precision which places the best of these agiba among the finest works from the Gulf.

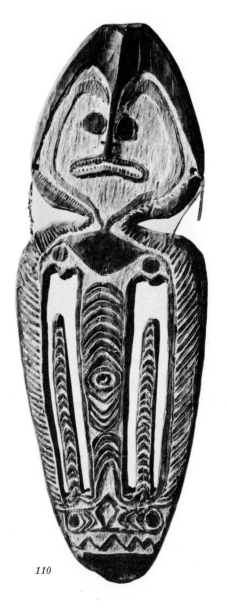

110

111

112, 113

108 *Agiba with human skulls. Dopima, 1930. 109 Agiba with human skulls and pig's jawbone, in ceremonial house. Peltumuba, 1912. 110 Agiba. Coll. P. Wirz, 1930: old work. Wood, black, red, white paint, 34¼" long. Collection Mr. and Mrs. Gustave Schindler. 111 Agiba. British Museum. 112 Agiba with animal skull. Coll. P. Wirz, 1930. Wood, paint, 20½" long. Amsterdam 2670–291. 113 Agiba (na-agiba) with bird, reptile and fish bones. Coll. P. Wirz, 1930. Wood, 21¼" long*

KEREWA AREA

The most numerous objects from the Kerewa are the gope
boards. The outline is generally a more or less broad oval.
A slight convexity is due to their being cut from old canoes.
They range in size from some nine feet to less than three feet
in length. The designs are in relief; the depth varies, it is said
(though Austen and Wirz disagree on how) according to the
class of the board. The raised surfaces are painted (not
charred, apparently) black. The sunk grounds are painted in
white and a range of "reds" which includes pink, red ochre,
and ochres verging on shades of orange. These colors are not
always, strangely enough, logically disposed as infillings of
the spaces. In some instances, two colors appear on the same
ground in a way which could have been avoided by reversing
the colors. Such a reversal was not traditionally impossible, as
at least one gope shows.

Few of the gope have any more definite provenience than
"Goaribari"; this may, of course, apply either to the village
itself, or to the whole island with its several villages. In any
case, the designs exist in several styles, basic elements of which
are variously combined. It would be interesting to allocate
them geographically, but the somewhat negative evidence
would rather indicate that these were concurrent at least on
Goaribari Island.

A large proportion—perhaps half—of those known appear
to share a single, very specific style. In nearly every case it is
carried out with a strictness worthy of the agiba style, and the
boards themselves are very regular in form, with pointed ends.
The most important feature of the figures carved on these
boards is the head, which as usual consists of a widow's peak
connected by a straight ridge to a V-shaped mouth and round

eyes. The eyes are at the base of long, inverted triangular
forms, the vertices of which are connected by ridges to the
outer corners of the brow shape. The space between them is
often filled with a long diamond (for the nostrils) which
unites the whole design.

The trunk is a circle-and-chevron unit, from which thin
limbs extend in a somewhat feebly stated hocker position. The

58

119

120   121   122

legs are sometimes so jointed that they surround an X-shaped space: often this is cut through the board. A common method of balancing this at the top of the board is a pair of incurving ridges describing the same shape, which again may be pierced. Alternatively the ridges are detached from the border of the gope and completed as pointed ovals, which in their turn may be pierced.

A few gope boards incorporating this face convention show interesting variations. In one example, the head is surrounded by a number of rings. In two other "ringed" examples, the figure is reduced to the head and the trunk unit; except for a border, the field is plain. Rare in the Kerewa culture area, this scheme is the most westerly example of the typical layout of Namau kwoi boards.

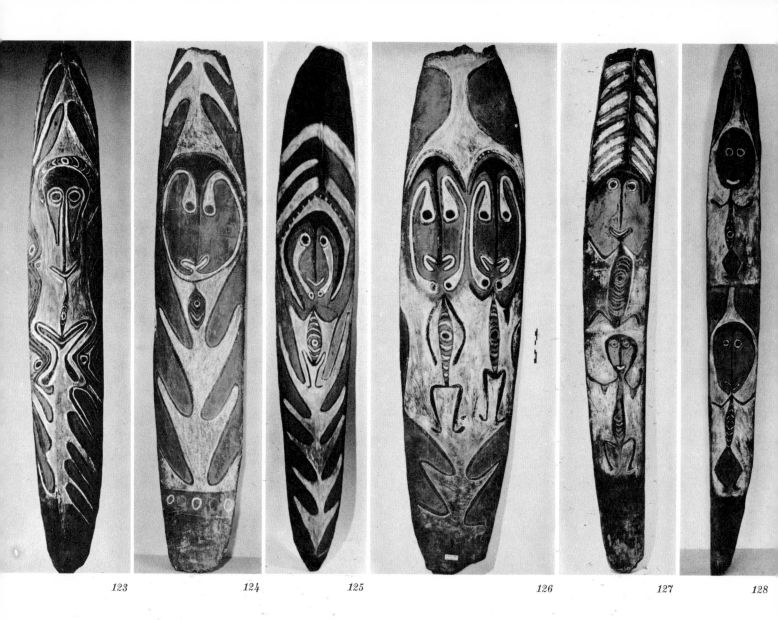

123   124   125   126   127   128

130   131

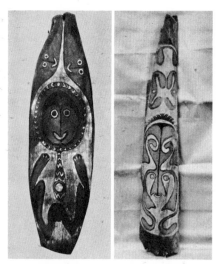

Gope are also designed in several other styles. In these the board itself tends to be less regular; some indeed have crudely chopped-off or even straight ends. The most important of these styles is immediately striking for its spontaneity and freedom, in contrast to the tension of that just described. Its vitality derives from the special personality given by the design of the heads, and the movement of the border designs. For, in these gope, the pointed oval forms are developed into (or merely replaced by) rows of loops, connected to the edge of the board, which are often stated as a continuous flowing line. The heads of the figures on these boards have inverted triangles depending from the eyes, but these sometimes curve up, then outwards. When they join at the "chin," it is worth noticing that not only the face becomes a unit, but that the form of the unit has particular interest. Since the nose and mouth are summarily expressed by a double V open below, the face develops into four incurving forms, two up, two down, which themselves resemble in sum a hocker figure.

60

129

134

135

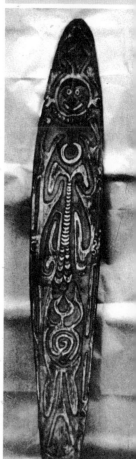

114–122 *Ancestral boards (gope or kaiaimunu). Kerewa area: 114 Basel Vb 14012. 115 Coll. P. Wirz, 1930. Paint, 56½" high. Basel Vb 8035. 116 Coll. P. Wirz, 1930. Paint, 57⅞" high. Amsterdam 2670–279. 117 Col. A. B. Lewis, 1912. Fibre tassels, 46¾" high. Chicago 142703. 118 Coll. Cook Daniels, 1905. Paint. British Museum 1906.10.13.283. 119 Coll. Cook Daniels, 1905. About 108" high. British Museum. 120 Coll. A. B. Lewis, 1912. Paint. Chicago. 121 Coll. A. B. Lewis, 1912. Paint, fibre tassels, 59" high. Chicago 142705. 122 Coll. Cook Daniels, 1905. Paint. British Museum 1906.10.13.278. 123 Coll. P. Wirz, 1930. Amsterdam 2670–278. 124 Goaribari. Coll. Bradley Patten, 1912. Red, black and white paint, 68" high. Collection Mr. Ralph Altman. 125 Coll. A. B. Lewis, 1912. Red, black and white paint, 57" high. Chicago 142706. 126 Paiya. Coll. A. C. Haddon, 1914. 46¼" high. Cambridge 1916.143.41. 127 Coll. P. Wirz, 1930. 66¾" high. Collection Mr. Heker Jensen. 128 Coll. P. Wirz, 1930. 83⅜" high. Basel Vb 7765. 129 Coll. Cook Daniels, 1905. British Museum 1906.10.13.277. 130 Coll. Cook Daniels, 1905. British Museum 1906.10.13.282. 131 Coll. Cook Daniels, 1905. British Museum 1906.10.13.275. 132 Coll. A. B. Lewis, 1912. 26¾" high. Chicago 142708. 133 Coll. A. B. Lewis, 1912. 20⅞" high. Chicago 142709. 134 Coll. A. B. Lewis, 1912. 54¼" high. Chicago 142707. 135 British Museum, about 72" high*

132   133

In a further group, the eyes are entirely without this elaboration, and the bodies reduced to matchstick proportions. The flowing borders are similarly reduced to broad lobes. Some gope which may be included in this group, on the basis of the face design, are highly eccentric in their freedom. A few gope seem to be totally individual in conception. They must be distinguished from yet another group in fluent and decisive designs which are atypical for the Kerewa area but have much in common with the typical gope of the Wapo-Era district. The question of which influenced which is insoluble and perhaps hardly germane, but the style does not seem native to Kerewa, and these examples must be recalled later in terms of the Wapo-Era gope.

The "spontaneous" gope styles find their closest affinity in a different class of objects, in which we may perhaps discern the spirit prompting them. To see this in its purest essence, we must examine the mysterious imunu objects which are used from Kerewa to Purari Delta. As has been said, these are no more and no less than naturally formed pieces of wood which strike the tribesmen as the abodes of supernatural powers. They are, in fact, the Gulf equivalent of *objets trouvés,* with a westerner's aesthetic sensibility magnified by a more direct sense of magic. That an aesthetic choice is involved—however unconsciously—we cannot doubt.

Many human figures from the area look like, and probably are, a developed stage of the imunu. The kakame are certainly natural pieces of wood (like the usual imunu) elaborated into carvings. The more definitely human figures from the Turama River to Wapo Creek are still virtually natural fragments of wood with figures in relief on the surface. The head is usually disengaged; a fork of the branch is adapted for legs in the kakame figures. The torso is represented, in the Turama-Goaribari area, by the conventional circle-and-chevron design. The arms and legs are often posed in the conventional gesture of the gope boards, but are here almost embryonic, in proportion. Otherwise the limbs hang straight down. The faces are also in the familiar gope pattern, more or less strictly adhered to. A few of the dancing clubs or imitation trophy heads are powerful skull-like images.

Their spontaneity gives each of these carvings a peculiar vitality. There can be no doubt that they are the most personal works of art from the whole Papuan Gulf area. In no others does individual genius transform the stocks and billets which are the material into creatures not the less fascinating because they still possess a quality of accidental discovery.

The same quality is found in the stools and headrests adapted from natural formations. They are customarily ornamented at one end with engravings of human heads: one rare specimen has a head of remarkable naturalism, others have the usual conventionalized face. Their resemblance to animal forms is perhaps fortuitous, and would not occur to their makers. In any case, the unedited crudity of their material is itself the source of their rhetoric.

137

136

136 Figure. Goaribari. Coll. A. B. Lewis, 1912. Wood, paint, fibre, 40⅛" total height. Chicago 142716. 137 Carved log. Paiya. Coll. P. Wirz, 1930. Wood, paint, 25⅝" high. Basel 8052. 138 Stick figure (imunu). Era Delta: Gibi. Coll. P. Wirz, 1930. Root, 16½" high. Basel Vb 7767. 139 Figure (kakame), personal name Burio. Wapo Creek. Coll. P. Wirz, 1930. Natural tree fork, paint, 31½" high. Amsterdam 2670–300. 140 Male figure. Wapo. Coll. P. Wirz, 1930. Part of tree, red and white paint, shell ornaments, bag, 37⅜" high. Amsterdam 2670–299. 141 Headrest. Goaribari. Coll. A. B. Lewis, 1912. Wood, red, white, black paint. Chicago 142662. 142, 143 Stool. Humobawi. Wood, paint, 43¼" long. Amsterdam 2670–295

141

142

143

140

138

139

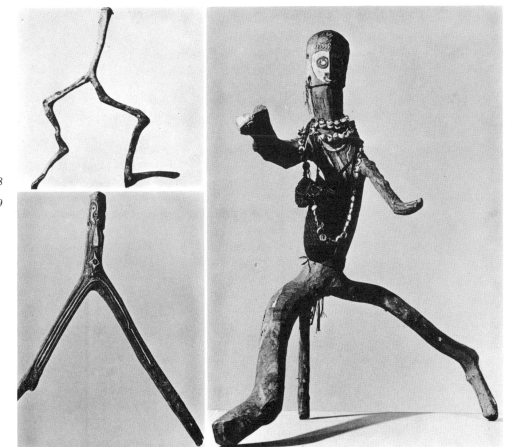

144a

144b

144 a, b Imitation trophy head. Wapo. Coll. P. Wirz, 1930. Light wood, traces white paint, 7⅝″ high. Museum of Primitive Art 60.89. 145, 146 Imitation trophy head. Wapo? Wood, cowrie shells, white paint, 13″ high. Collection Mr. and Mrs. R. J. Sainsbury

147 Dance club. Kerewa area, Gefbari. Coll. P. Wirz, 1930. Wood, 20⅞″ high. Basel Vb 7871

147

146

151

WAPO CREEK

The stools and kakame figures of the Wapo Creek which share the peculiar spontaneity of those from Kerewa have this quality enhanced, if anything, by the decorative elements which appear on them. They also figure on the gope of the area. But where the spontaneity of Kerewa objects often derives from the relaxation of what is, ideally, a tight and intellectual style, the style itself of Wapo Creek objects is based on an intuitive placing of conventional elements. To see this most clearly it is only necessary to return to those Kerewa gope which are closest in style and to notice their comparative rigidity and the artist's apparent compulsion to fill the whole field with a continuous design.

The conventional elements themselves consist of isolated linear forms, the commonest being a circle from which four spirals branch diagonally; this occurs in two major variations, distinguished by the spirals' direction of torque. Undoubtedly formalizations of the torso and limbs, such forms occur on the gope boards below a very characteristic small face of which the general outline is an inverted triangle or heart shape, with small round eyes and nostrils, and a rather small mouth. The outlines of the boards decorated in this style vary considerably; probably they are not considered as fundamentally important to it. The essential, the disposition of the designs, is carried out with an unforced sureness. In some boards the designs are actually connected and so assembled as to create an

152

upward-bouncing, springy composition. This sense of movement is typical of this area, but otherwise unique in Papuan Gulf art. It is shared with the designs on a mask and is expressed again by the small bioma figures of the area in their upraised arms.

153

154

148–152 Ancestral boards (gope): 148 Coll. P. Wirz, 1930. Wood, paint, 31½" high. Amsterdam 2670–273. 149 Meagama. Coll. John Vandercook, 1929. Wood, white, ochre and black paint; 42½" high. Brooklyn 51.118.6. 150 Coll. P. Wirz, 1930. Wood, paint, 44½" high. Amsterdam 2670–267. 151 Coll. P. Wirz, 1930. Wood, paint, 42½" high. Amsterdam 2670–269. 152 Meagama. Coll. John Vandercook, 1929. Wood, paint, 53" high. Brooklyn 51.118.5. 153 Ancestral boards (gope) in a Wapo area men's house, 1930. 154 Mask (keweke). Bark cloth, cane; red, black and white paint, 66⅞" high. Basel Vb 7838

WAPO CREEK

155 Figure (bioma). Coll. P. Wirz, 1930. Wood, paint, fibre, 15⅜" high. Amsterdam 2670–287. 156 Figure (bioma). Coll. P. Wirz, 1930. Wood, white and red paint, 22" high. Basel Vb 7868. 157 Figure (bioma). Coll. P. Wirz, 1930. Wood, white and red paint, 18½" high. 158 Figure (bioma). Coll. P.

155   156   157   158

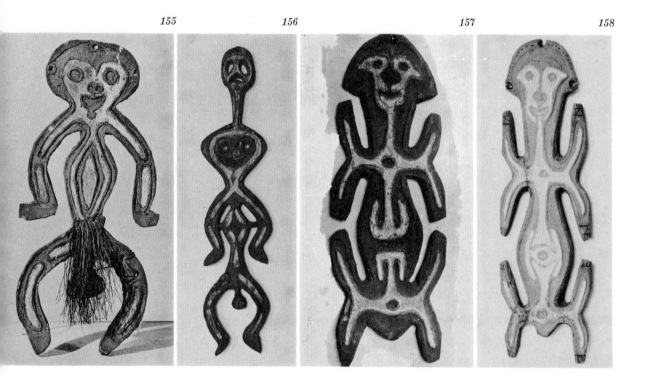

159

Wirz, 1930. Wood, paint. Basel Vb 8003. 159 Bioma with associated pig skulls in Wapo area men's house, 1930. 160 Figure (bioma). Meagama. Coll. John Vandercook, 1929. Wood, black and white paint, 25⅛" high. Brooklyn 51.118.8. 161 Male figure (bioma), of Ipiawo clan? Coll. P. Wirz

161

160

162 *Figure (Irivake). Era—Maipua River district. Coll. P. Wirz, 1930. Wood, fibre, bark belt, red and white paint, 50" high. Amsterdam 2670–282.* 163 *Figure (agiba). Era River district. Coll. P. Wirz, 1930. Wood, white and red paint, 40½" high. Amsterdam 2670–283.* 164 *Male figure (bioma). Era River delta. Coll. P. Wirz, 1930. Wood, paint, 20⅞" high. Amsterdam 2670–284.* 165 *Male figure (bioma). Era River delta. Wood, paint, 16⅜" high. Amsterdam 2670–286.* 166 *Ancestral board (gope). Tetehui. Bark, paint, 37⅝" high. Amsterdam 2670–276.* 167 *Ancestral board (gope). Tetehui. Coll. P. Wirz, 1930. Bark, paint, 33½" high. Amsterdam 2149–17.* 168 *Male figure (bioma). Koiravi. Coll. John Vandercook, 1929. Wood, black, white, red ochre paint, 26½" high. Brooklyn 51. 118.9*

163   164

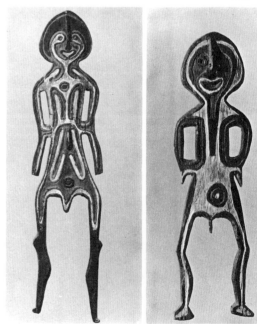

168

ERA RIVER

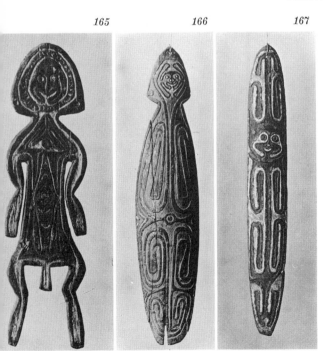

165   166   167

These figures sometimes, interestingly enough, have two sets of limbs, one upraised, one lowered. Characteristically, they have raised edges along the outer sides, connected with bridges at the knee and elbow joints. One such figure is extraordinarily complex and sophisticated in the interplay of its eight opposing limbs and the designs imposed over them and the torso. Usually these figures are flat; the movement of this one is enhanced by its being cut from a curved slab (again, probably part of an old canoe). It is the work of an exceptionally talented artist. Besides this, however, the vitality of this bioma is not only unusual in itself, but apparently exceptional for the Era River district from which it comes. A large figure, for all its ambitious size, is a good deal stiffer. That this is not merely due to the individual artist may be seen in other Era River bioma, where the Wapo conventional patterns have stiffened into plain hook shapes, and the figures themselves are not only symmetrical but static. Indeed, it even seems that the Era bioma have lowered arms, in contrast to the upraised ones of Wapo. As a subdivision of the area, the gope made from sheets of bark at Tetehui village have a consistent form in which heads with necks are distinguished at the upper ends, and the ornamentation consists entirely of a vertical arrangement of the plain hooks.

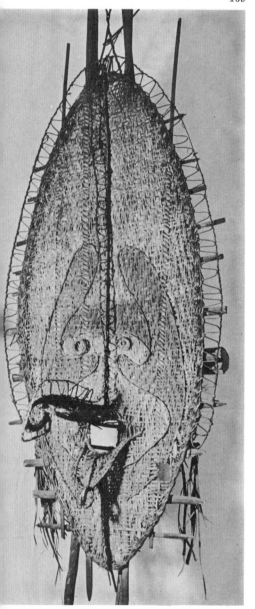

169   170

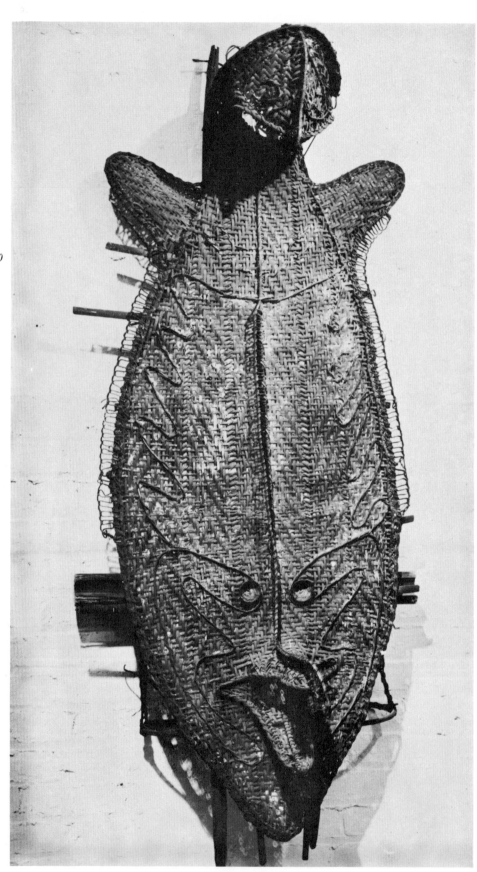

The masks of the area, both of the kanipu round-head variety and the tall oval keweke, are made with considerable elaboration. The kanipu are built up on rather heavy rings of cane. They consequently have a regularity in their domed crania which, combined with the stubbiness of the open jaws, imparts a certain stiff ferocity. The keweke masks differ in character from those of Urama, or the aiaimunu and hevehe, by having their faces set relatively high in the field of the mask: a successful stratagem, which gives each face importance as part of the composition rather than as a pendant to a great decorative panel.

The patterns on the masks are outlined in strips of cane: some masks are sheeted in bark cloth, others have paint applied directly to the basketry surface. The designs on the keweke masks have a marked similarity to those of the gope boards; the smaller-scale designs on the kanipu, on the other hand, seem condensed versions of those of the Urama keweke. Both types of mask, in the Era district, are often ornamented along edges and median brow lines with undulating strips of rattan which are intended to be trimmed with feathers. It is interesting that the kaiaimunu are decorated in the same way, and that the kanipu, which are apparently worn by young boys, have small crests also found on the basketry animals. One unusual kanipu actually bears a strong resemblance to a kaiaimunu head. There seems to be a connection here between the kanipu and kaiaimunu animals, with a hint of the masking of initiates as an analogue of the Namau Pairama ceremony.

The mysterious basketry objects called ubudubu (= "schlechtes Ding": Wirz 1934:84) cannot be elucidated, but must be mentioned. They are associated with the kaiaimunu, but appear to take mask form; one at least resembles the loop-nosed Kerewa avoko masks.

171, 172

173

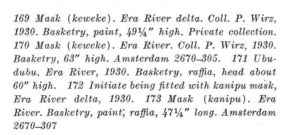

169 Mask (keweke). Era River delta. Coll. P. Wirz, 1930. Basketry, paint, 49¼" high. Private collection. 170 Mask (keweke). Era River. Coll. P. Wirz, 1930. Basketry, 63" high. Amsterdam 2670–305. 171 Ubudubu. Era River, 1930. Basketry, raffia, head about 60" high. 172 Initiate being fitted with kanipu mask, Era River delta, 1930. 173 Mask (kanipu). Era River. Basketry, paint, raffia, 47¼" long. Amsterdam 2670–307

174

176   177

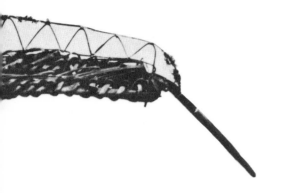

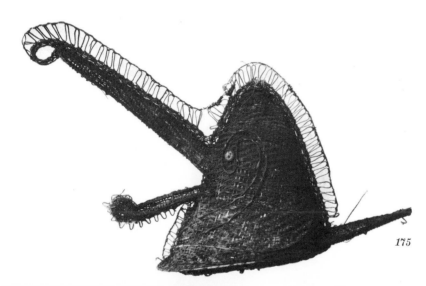

174 Kaiaimunu animal, Purari Delta. Coll. P. Wirz, 1930. Basketry, about 120″ long. Basel Vb 8070. 175 Mask (kanipu). Era River, Raviwana. Coll. P. Wirz, 1930. Rattan, 27½″ high. Basel Vb 7835. 176, 177 Kaiaimunu animals in Era River men's houses, 1930

175

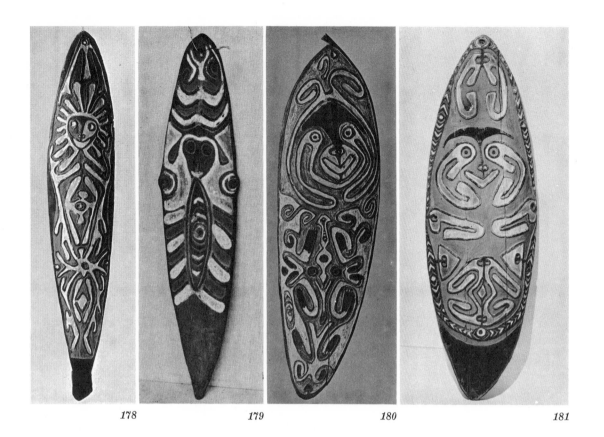

178   179   180   181

ERA RIVER

URAMA

*178–181 Era River gope, coll. P. Wirz, 1930. 178 Wood, paint, 65"
high. Amsterdam 2670–271. 179 Wood, paint. Basel. 180 Wood,
paint, 57½" high. Amsterdam 2670–261. 181 Wood, yellow, black,
white paint, 57⅛" high. Collection Mr. Serge Brignoni*

182–185 Masks at Urama, 1924

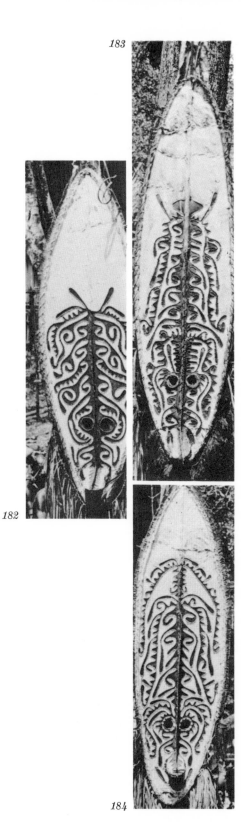

183

182

184

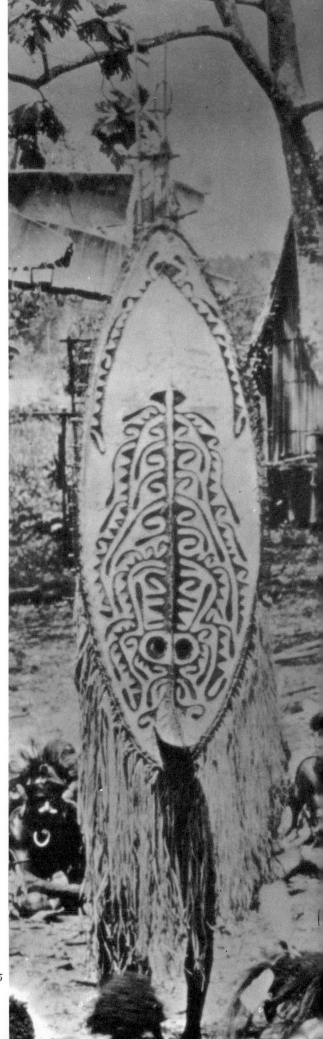

The most striking works from Urama are the large oval masks. As on the gope, the designs stand out against a large blank oval surface, sometimes bordered or partly bordered with small patterns. The designs themselves come from the midrib of the mask in the form of hooks or curves, or single-turn spirals or short connecting lines. Interspersed with these are lines with saw-toothed edges: perhaps a reminiscence of the favorite Kiwai diamond patterns, they will appear in much greater profusion to the west.

185

187

186

186 Masks (kanipu?) in an Urama men's house, 1924. 187–189
Gope from Urama. Coll. P. Wirz, 1930. Wood, paint: 187 Amsterdam 2670–268. 188 49¼" high, Basel Vb 8025. 189 42⅞"
high, Amsterdam 2670–266. 190–192 Gope with pig trophy
skulls in Urama men's house, 1924

188   189 190 191

192

The gope of Urama Island are well documented by field photographs. They appear to be shaped to a remarkably uniform pattern: a regular, long oval tapering at the ends. A human face always occurs about the middle of the board, sometimes with a prominent nose, as in one group of Wapo examples. The rest of the field is carried out in at least two schemes. The first is interesting in that it appears to combine the conventionalized figure designs with hook forms coming in horizontally from the edges. These may be compared with those of the Tetehui style, but may also be construed as a version of the flowing line borders of Kerewa gope. In the other scheme (probably the commoner) the gope is bordered by a band of chevrons in each quadrant: numerous variations are played

on this, of course. A remarkable number of repetitions of gope designs seem to occur in Urama: in three photographs of cubicles, four examples of one design in a single design occur; five of a second design in another cubicle, and three more of this same design in another.

The elegant aspect of work from Urama can hardly be overstressed. It is precise, contained, and disciplined towards decorativeness to a degree which makes it contrast sharply with the immediately neighboring styles. Part of the effect of unity it conveys probably derives from the close correspondence between the motives, and their arrangement, found on the gope and the masks. This correspondence also exists in Wapo, but perhaps in no other areas of the Gulf.

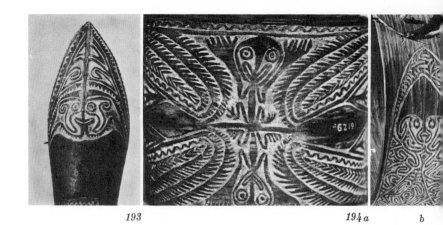

193   194a   b

COASTAL NAMAU

197
196   198

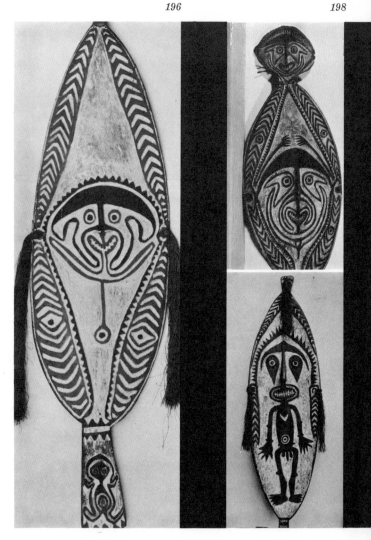

The art of the Purari Delta shares with that of the Elema tribes the distinction of being the first of the Gulf styles to become generally known in Europe. Being both portable and spectacular, the ancestral boards have found their way into museums in very considerable numbers. They must indeed have always been very numerous, as both field photographs and a simple calculation may show. If Ukiravi had eight ravi, each with about ten larava, each of these holding six to ten kwoi; then it seems likely that in this village alone there must have been between five hundred and a thousand kwoi at any one time. It seems quite certain that the material on hand represents only a small proportion of the styles that must have existed.

The fact that a belt of originally western immigrants settled themselves along the coast line from Vaimuru to Maipua led to the formation of a very definite group of styles. It is most noticeable in the kwoi, particularly those coming from Maipua. These are indeed what might be thought of as the classic type for the area, and in fact some of this kind are made in Iari. Characteristically it tends to be a broad oval with a long flat tab at the foot. The border is a chevron strip in four sections; there is a large face in the middle, the brow being particularly stressed, and the eyes set in the midst of elaborate designs. The whole aspect is quite similar to that of the gope of Urama: but here the designs are carried out in rather thin black lines on a white background; and above all, the total effect is not only simple but often violent.

Many other styles exist, of course, but in such variety that it is hardly possible to generalize. It seems likely however that in Kaimari considerable invention was displayed with a more copious use of the three basic colors (red, black, and white) and of the saw-toothed line as a decorative element.

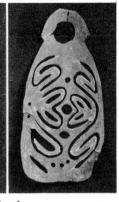
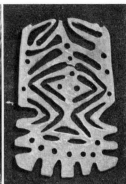

c   195a b

200   201

193 Drum. Wood, paint, 38" high. Auckland 6114. 194a Belt. Bark, paint. Philadelphia P 4143. 194b Belt. Orokolo Bay or Purari Delta. Bark, raffia, cowrie shell, terra cotta paint, lime, 3⅜" wide. Museum of Primitive Art 59.142. 194c Belt. Bark, terra cotta paint, lime, 4½" wide. Museum of Primitive Art 56.72. 195a Earring. Maipua. Tortoise shell. Buffalo C 11283. 195b Earring. Maipua. Tortoise shell, 3⅛" high. Buffalo C 11272. 196 Kwoi. Wood, red, black and white paint; red fibre tassels; 42" high. Buffalo C 8178. 197 Kwoi. Maipua? Wood, paint, 43¼" high. Edinburgh 1951. 368. 198 Kwoi. Wood, red, black and white paint; fibre tassels, 57⅜" high. Hamburg 3580:07. 199 Kwoi. Kaimari. Coll. A. B. Lewis, 1912. Wood, paint. Chicago 142409. 200 Clubs (aviya). Maipua or lari. Wood, red, black and white paint. 34", 27", 13", 29" high. From Webster, 1911. 201 Dance staff (aviya). Wood, red, black and white paint; 13¾" high. From Webster, 1911. 202 Comb. Wood, red and white paint, 10" by 12". Buffalo C 9493

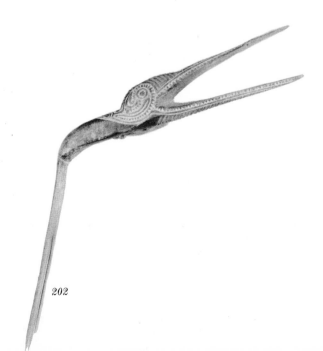

202

203

The masks are notable for the great symmetry of their designs, which appear to be arranged upward on repetitive sectors which are more regular than those of Urama. In those of Kaimari the saw tooth is used up the midrib of the aiaimunu, and in both Kaimari and Maipua it frequently borders the mask design elements. The down-drooping tendency of some of these is extremely prolonged in the Kaimari mask style. Kaimari and Maipua seem to produce sophisticated work; Kerewa, near Maipua, has in contrast a much simpler, even broader style.

While it is true that masks and kwoi share a few characteristics—brow "thundercloud" pads, like those of the kaiaimunu animals, and a use of black designs on a white field—there is otherwise little congruity of style between them. The kwoi boards, on the other hand, are distinctly closer to the type of carving found on drums and bull-roarers: an interesting distinction is that the use of a particular design is obviously based on the type of material used. It may be noticed, however, that the designs on such relatively small objects as drums, hairpins, dance-wands, spoons, and bark belts, are usually much closer-knit than those of the kwoi. As some of these things at least are used for ceremonial gifts or exchanges, perhaps a conscious element of virtuosity is involved.

203 Masks in Kerewa (?) men's house, 1930. Masks (kanipu). Purari Delta. Cane; bark cloth; red, black and white paint: 204 28"high. 205 36" high. 206 26" high. From Webster, 1911. 207 Mask. Kerewa. Coll. P. Wirz, 1930. Cane; bark cloth; red, black and white paint; 49¼" high. Basel Vb 7829. 208 Interior of Kaimari men's house, 1924. 209 Interior of Kaimari men's house, 1930

COASTAL NAMAU

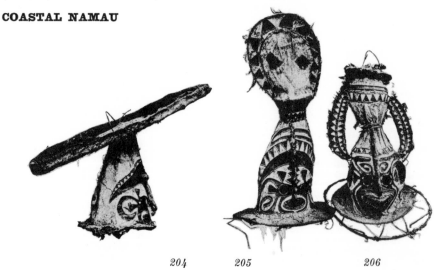

204   205   206

208

209

A somewhat bland type of figure sculpture occurs in the coastal area. These full figures, or small heads, have fire-blackened surfaces with details added in startling contrast in red and white. They are distinguished by large horizontal drop-shaped eyes, and wide crescentic mouths with saw teeth. Sometimes their would-be naturalism is enhanced by wigs and bark belts.

Bark cloth is also used to construct small figures, or as sheeting over a wooden base for some larger figures. Since the wood is uncarved, these again are perhaps also imunu. These constructions are hardly works of art at all, though they have a hideous vitality. One, from Ukiravi, is indeed notable in its gruesomeness, and shows the very real difference between that quality and the artfully achieved forcefulness of much Gulf art.

210

211a b

214   215

216

212 213

217

COASTAL NAMAU

*210 Imitation trophy head (kopuku). Maipua. Wood;
red, black and white paint. From Webster, 1911. 211a, b
Imitation trophy head. Wood; red, black and white paint.
Basel Vb 14025. 212 Male figure. Ikunu. Coll. P. Wirz,
1930. Wood, red and white paint, 70⅞" high. Basel Vb
7784. 213 Female figure. Ikunu. Coll. P. Wirz, 1930.
Scorched wood, fiber, red and white paint, 59" high. Basel
Vb 7785. 214 Animal figure (imunu). Coll. P. Wirz,
1930. Wood, paint, 59¾" long. Basel Vb 7855. 215 Bird
(imunu). Ukiravi. Coll. P. Wirz, 1930. Burl wood, paint,
16½" high. Basel Vb 7875. 216 Headrest. Kaimari.
Wood, white paint. Chicago 142432. 217 Dog. Maipua.
Bark cloth, paint. Cambridge 1916.143.204*

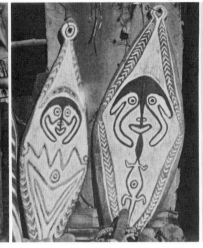

218 219 220 221

223

218–221 Kwoi. Wood, paint. In men's houses at: 218 Kairu, 1912. 219, 220 Ukiravi, 1912. 221 Kwoi. Ukiravi. Coll. P. Wirz, 1930. 40⅛" high. Basel Vb 7847. 222 Six Kwoi. Iari? Coll. James Chalmers, probably 1883. British Museum. 223 Figure. Ukiravi (from "Omai's ravi"). Coll. A. C. Haddon, 1914. Human skull, wood, bamboo, rattan, bark cloth, swordfish snout, bark, cowrie shell, cassowary feathers. Cambridge Z 9372372. 224 Imitation trophy head. Coll. P. Wirz, 1930. Cane; bark cloth; red, black and white paint; 18⅛" long. Collection Mr. Serge Brignoni. 225 Skull of "Kapara-ipi, a man of Aivari." Cane, feathers, cowrie shell, brown and black paint on clay. British Museum (Beasley Coll.) 1944. Oc 2. 1939. 226 Face paint designs from fig. 225

The inland Namau styles of kwoi are roughly distinguishable from those of the Kaimari by the shape of the board. They have a tendency to a diamond outline, sometimes rather high-shouldered. The borders are probably preponderantly the usual bands of chevrons, but they also include the angular patterns carved along the gunwales of canoes (this feature also occurs on some Kaimari masks). The eye designs of the faces trail downward, often as a filler for the lower part of the field, as on some gope from the immediate west. This area is otherwise sometimes occupied by various designs, some of which are a simple version of the typical Wapo-Era design, while others seem to represent crocodiles or lizards. The Ukiravi boards are mainly black-line-on-white, but a group from Iari shows an especial richness in the arrangement of color as well as an elaboration of the animal figures.

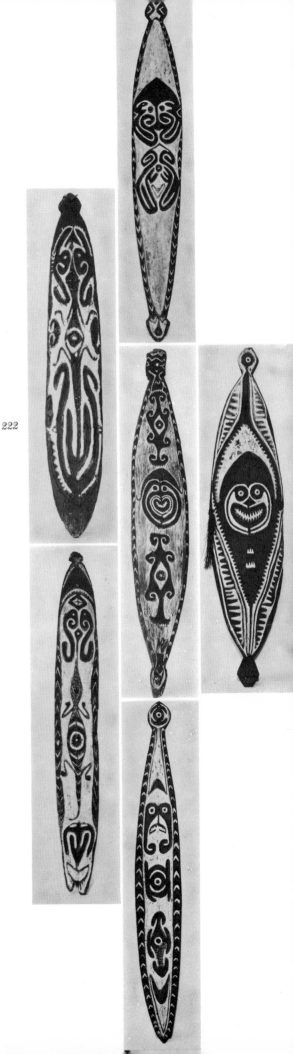

222

224 225

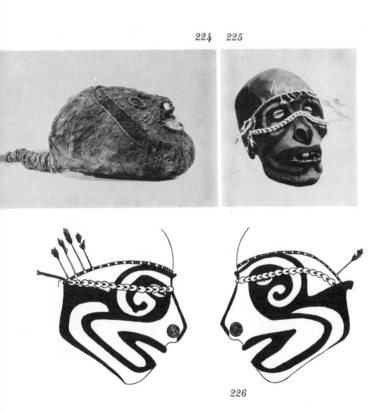

226

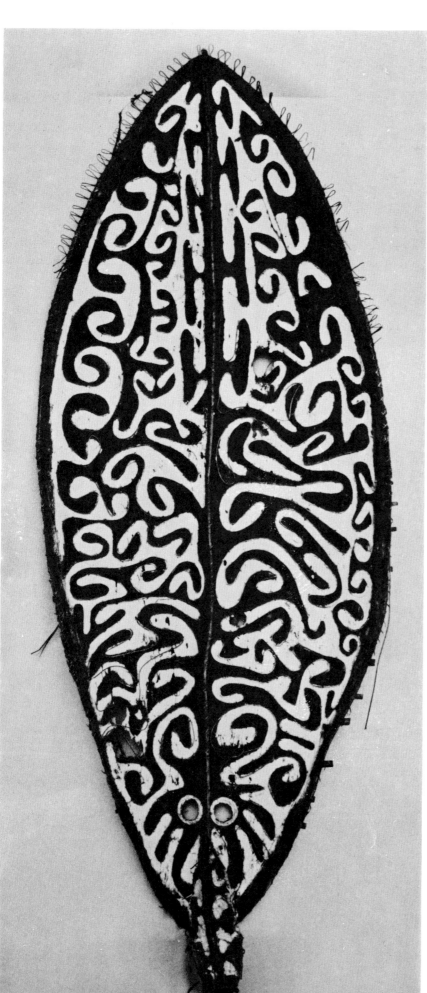

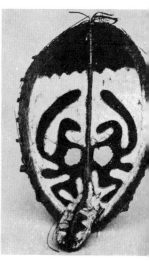

230

228

227

88

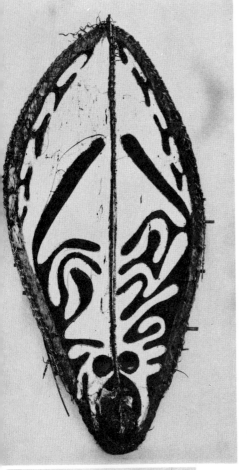

229

INLAND NAMAU

The masks show the same kind of divergence from the kwoi styles that has been discussed for the coastal areas. In this area the large aiaimunu masks have totally asymmetrical decoration, the individual elements being elaborated or abridged at will, and connected willy-nilly to the outside rim, the border, or each other. Only on the small kanipu are the designs regular: here they are simple eye designs.

Masks (aiaimunu). In-
land Namau. Coll. be-
fore 1890. Cane, bark
cloth, black and white
paint. 227 96" high.
Dublin 351:90. 228
26" high. Dublin 348:
90. 229 Formerly col-
lection Paul Eluard.
230 48" high. Dublin
349:90. Painted bark
figures attached to
ravi posts: 231 Ko-
riki. Coll. A. B. Lewis,
1912. Red and white,
23⅝" high. Chicago
142425. 232 Koriki.
Coll. A. B. Lewis, 1912.
Black and white,
30¾" high. Chicago
142426. 233. Ukiravi
("Kara-arabi's ravi").
Coll. A. C. Haddon.
17⅛" high. Cambridge
16.143.191. 234 Uki-
ravi ("Omai's ravi").
Coll. A. C. Haddon.
40⅝" high. Cambridge
16.143.182

231   232   233   234

235

The hevehe masks of Orokolo and the district around it depart sharply from the Western styles. Here the midrib is the focus for a vertically symmetrical arrangement of the aualari patterns—elements which, as has been said, are representations of natural forms such as plants of many varieties, parts of animals, and even sea foam. The eyes are surrounded with elaborate barbed patterns with extensions upward which immediately recall the raised arms of the western gope and other objects. East of Orokolo, however, the over-all design reverts to the western style—a fact possibly explained through Williams' belief (1940:395) that certain factors in the present Orokolo form of Hevehe are modern. In the masks from Kerema (Uaripi tribe), although the mask patterns are both curvilinear and unified into large designs, they are also detached from both the midrib and the eye ports. Among the Toaripi of Motumotu, still farther to the west, the masks follow the Urama and Kaimari fashion of having the patterns spring from the midrib; and the patterns themselves are the closest to those of Urama in the whole Elema area.

The Namau have acquired ritual elements from the Elema of Orokolo, and a small mask from Maipua is clearly a hevehe.

235 Masks (hevehe). Orokolo, 1930.   236 Mask (semese). Kerema. Coll. A. B. Lewis, 1912. Chicago.   237 Mask (hevehe). Maipua. 47½" high. Q.M. E.13. 226. From Harris, 1913.   238, 239 Masks (semese). Kiri, 1912.   240 Masks (semese). Motumotu. Berlin

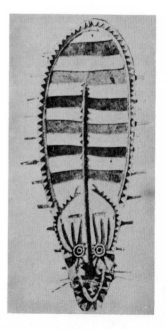

237

236

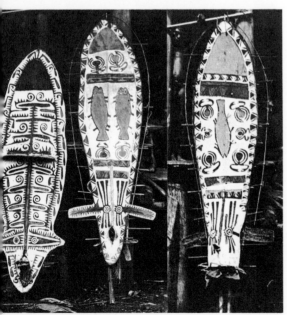

238, 239

240

241, 242

243, 244, 245

246, 247, 248

249

241 Hohao. Orokolo, 1912. 242 Right: Figure (hohao). Wood; sienna, white and umber paint, 33½" high. Buffalo C 8185. Left: Hohao. Wood; sienna, white and umber paint, 36½" high. Buffalo C 8183. 243 Hohao. Wood, paint. Art Institute of Chicago. 244 Hohao. Vailala? Coll. before 1890. Wood, paint, fibre tassels, 61" high. Dublin 339:90. 245 Hohao. Coll. before 1890. Wood, paint, fibre tassels, 55½" high. Dublin 334:90. 246 Hohao. Kerema? Coll. before 1890. Wood, paint, 47⅝" high. Dublin 338:90. 247 Hohao. Kerema? Wood, paint, 55⅞" high. Manchester 05790. 248 Hohao. Wood, paint. Brooklyn 02.111. 249 Figure (hohao). Wood, paint, fibre tassels, 29½" high. Rautenstrauch-Joest Museum 35764. 250 Figure (hohao). Wood; brown, red and white paint; 54⅛" high. Wellcome Historical Medical Museum 29.1952. 251 Canoe prow. Orokolo. Coll. A. B. Lewis, 1912. Wood, paint, 36¼" high. Chicago 142179. 252 Canoe prow. Orokolo. Coll. A. B. Lewis, 1912. Wood, paint, 40½" high. Chicago 142180. 253 Canoe prow. Coll. A. B. Lewis, 1912. Wood, paint. Chicago 142181

251   252   253

250

254 Shield. Kerema? Wood, paint, 28" high. Auckland 15463. 255 Shield. Wood, paint, 33½" high. Aberdeen 103.10. 256 Shield. Kerema? Wood, paint, 39" high. Hamburg E2483. 257 Shield. Kiri. Coll. A. B. Lewis, 1912. Wood, fibre, red and white paint. Chicago 142168. 258 Mask (eharo). Kerema. Coll. A. B. Lewis, 1912. Bark cloth, raffia, paint. Chicago 142116. 259 Mask (eharo). Cane; wood; fibre; black, red and white paint; 30" high. Collection Mr. and Mrs. Aaron Furman. 260 Mask (eharo). Orokolo. Bark cloth, cane, fibre, paint, feathers, 47¼" high. Blackwood, Coll., Oxford. 261 Mask. Orokolo. Coll. F. E. Williams. Cane; bark cloth; white, terra cotta, umber paint; raffia; 28¾" high. Museum of Primitive Art 58.309. 262 Mask. Motumotu. Cane, bark cloth, paint, fibre, 26¼" high. Peabody Museum, Harvard 50525

254   255
256   257

258

259

260

261

262

263

264

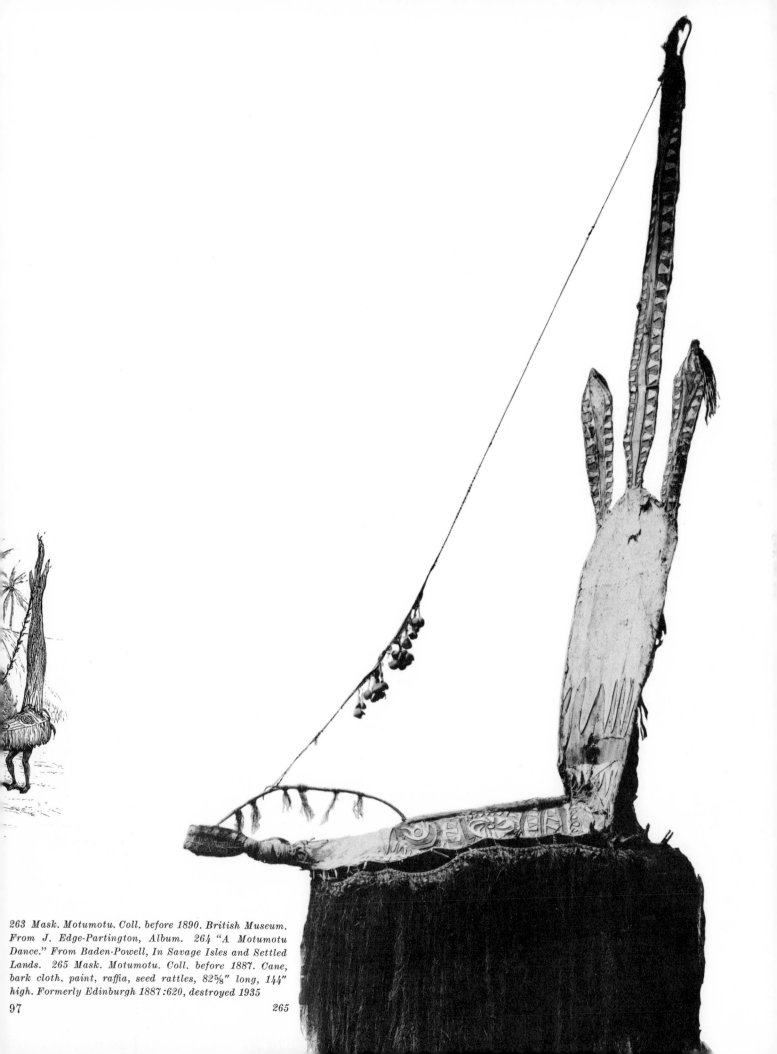

263 Mask. Motumotu. Coll. before 1890. British Museum. From J. Edge-Partington, Album. 264 "A Motumotu Dance." From Baden-Powell, In Savage Isles and Settled Lands. 265 Mask. Motumotu. Coll. before 1887. Cane, bark cloth, paint, raffia, seed rattles, 82⅝" long, 144" high. Formerly Edinburgh 1887:620, destroyed 1935

97   265

REFERENCES

Austen, Leo. 1932. Legends of Hido. Oceania, 2, 1931–32:468–475.

——. 1934. The dance of the gope in Kerewo. Man, 34, art. 3:4–8.

——. 1936. Head dances of the Turama River. Oceania, 6, 1935–36: 342–349.

——. 1947, 1948, 1950. Notes on the Turamarubi of western Papua. Mankind, 3, 1941–47:366–374; 4, 1948–54:14–23; 200–207.

Baden-Powell, B. F. S. 1892. In savage isles and settled lands. Malaysia, Australasia and Polynesia, 1888–1891. London.

Beaver, W. N. 1914. Some notes on the eating of human flesh in the western division of Papua. Man, 14, art. 74:145–147.

——. 1914. A description of the Girara district, western Papua. Geographical Journal, 43:407–413.

——. 1920. Unexplored New Guinea. Philadelphia.

Chalmers, James. 1887. Explorations in south-eastern New Guinea. Proceedings of the Royal Geographical Society, n.s., 9:71–81.

——. 1898. Toaripi. JRAI, 27:326–334.

Edge-Partington, James. 1890–98. An album of the weapons, tools, ornaments, articles of dress etc., of the natives of the Pacific islands. Manchester. 3 v.

Emst, P. van. 1958. In de ban der voorouders. Kunst uit Australisch Nieuw Guinea collectie P. Wirz. Amsterdam.

Flint, L. A. 1919. Muguru at Torobina, Bamu River. Man, 19, art. 19: 38–39.

Foy, W. 1902. Ethnographische Beziehungen zwischen Britisch-und Deutsch-Neu-Guinea. Globus, 82:379–383.

Haddon, A. C. 1894. The decorative art of British New Guinea. Dublin. (Royal Irish Academy. Cunningham memoirs, 10.)

——. 1918. The Agiba cult of the Kerewa culture. Man, 18, art. 99: 177–183.

——. 1919. The Kopiravi cult of the Namau, Papua. Man, 19, art. 91:177–179.

——. 1920. Migrations of cultures in British New Guinea. JRAI, 50:237–280.

——. 1947. Smoking and tobacco pipes in New Guinea. Philosophical transactions of the Royal Society of London, series B., 232:1–278.

—— and others. 1901–1935. Reports of the Cambridge anthropological expedition to Torres Straits. Cambridge. 6 v.

—— and James Hornell. 1936–1938. Canoes of Oceania. Honolulu. (Bernice P. Bishop Museum. Special publications, 27–29.)

Harris, R. Hamlyn. 1913. Some Papuan ceremonial appurtenances used at the Kaiva-Kuku and Semese dances. Queensland Museum memoirs, 2:9–24.

Holmes, J. H. 1924. In primitive New Guinea. London.

Hurley, Frank. 1924. Pearls and savages. New York.

Jukes, J. B. 1847. Narrative of the surveying voyage of H. M. S. Fly, commanded by Captain F. P. Blackwood, R.N. in Torres Strait, New Guinea, and other islands of the eastern archipelago, during the years 1842–1846. London, 2 v.

Kooijman, S. 1960. The art areas of western New Guinea. In Three areas of primitive art, by S. Kooijman, George Kubler and Hallam L. Movius Jr. New York.

Landtman, Gunnar. 1927. The Kiwai Papuans of British New Guinea. London.

——. 1933. Ethnographical collection from the Kiwai district of British New Guinea in the National Museum of Finland, Helsingfors (Helsinki). Helsinki.

Lewis, A. B. 1931. Carved and painted designs from New Guinea. Chicago. (Field Museum of Natural History. Anthropology design series, 5.)

Lyons, A. P. 1926. Notes on the Gogodara tribe of western Papua. JRAI, 56:329–359.

McCarthy, F. D. 1939. "Trade" in aboriginal Australia, and "trade" relationships with Torres Strait, New Guinea and Malaya. Oceania, 9, 1938–39:405–438; 10, 1939–40:80–104, 171–195.

Maher, Robert F. 1961. New men of Papua. Madison.

Murray, J. H. P. 1912. Papua, or British New Guinea. London.

Riley, E. Baxter. 1925. Among Papuan headhunters. London.

Seligmann, C. G. 1905. Notes on a painting on bark from the Aird River delta, British New Guinea. Man, 5, art. 89:161.

——. 1909. A classification of the natives of British New Guinea. JRAI, 39:246–275, 314–33.

——. 1910. The Melanesians of British New Guinea. Cambridge.

Spittal, R. H. 1906. Observations on fourteen New Guinea skulls. Proceedings of the Anatomical and Anthropological Society, University of Aberdeen, 1904–1906:88–95.

Vandercook, John W. 1937. Dark islands. New York.

*Webster, W. D. 1911. Catalogue of ethnographical specimens . . . no. 26. Leicester.

Williams, F. E. 1923. The Pairama ceremony in the Purari Delta, Papua. JRAI, 53:361–387.

——. 1924. The natives of the Purari Delta. Port Moresby. (Territory of Papua. Anthropology report, 5.)

——. 1936. Bull-roarers in the Papuan Gulf. (Government of Papua. Anthropology report, 17.)

——. 1939. The Kaiamunu–Ebiha–Gi cult in Papua. Man, 39, art. 50:48.

——. 1940. Drama of Orokolo. The social and ceremonial life of the Elema. Oxford.

Wirz, Paul. 1934. Beiträge zur Ethnographie des Papua-Golfes, Britisch-Neuguinea. Leipzig. (Museen für Tierkunde und Völkerkunde, Dresden. Abhandlungen und Berichte, 19.)

——. 1934a. Die Gemeinde der Gogodára. Leiden. (Nova Guinea, 16, livr. 4.)

——. 1934b. The social meaning of the sept-house and the sept-boat in Dutch and British New-Guinea. Tijdschrift voor Indische taal-, land- en volkenkunde, 74:140–148.

——. 1937. The Kaiamunu–Ebiha–Gi-cult in the Delta region and Western Division of Papua. JRAI, 67:407–413.

——. 1950. Der Ersatz für die Kopfjägerei und die Trophäen-imitation. In Beitrage zur Gesellungs- und Völkerwissenschaft, Professor Dr. Richard Thurnwald zu seinem achtzigsten Geburtstag gewidmet. [hrsg. von Ilse Tönnies] Berlin: 411–434.

CATALOGUE OF THE EXHIBITION

Revised descriptions in the catalogue should be preferred to those in the captions

TORRES STRAIT

1 *Rain charm (doiom). Mabuiag. Stone, 5¼" high. MPA 59.211*

2 *Mask. Erub. Turtle shell, human hair, 16⅛" high. MPA 59.106*

3 *Mask. Saibai? Wood, paint, string, cotton, shell, 19⅞" high. MPA 56.67*

4 *Dugong hunting charm? Torres Strait or lower Fly River. Wood, 24⅛" long. Collection Mr. Allan Frumkin. Ill. 58*

LOWER FLY RIVER

5 *Canoe board (gope). Tirio. Coll. A. B. Lewis, 1912. Wood; white, red, yellow ochre paint, fibre, 37" high. Chicago 142876. Ill. 11*

6 *Canoe board (gope). Tirio. Coll. A. B. Lewis, 1912. Wood; white, red, black paint, 40" high. Chicago 142877. Ill. 63*

7 *Canoe board (gope). Wood, red and white paint, 32⅜" high. Collection Mr. Allan Frumkin*

8 *Pendant figure (mimia). Wood, traces red and white paint, 13½" high. Collection Mr. and Mrs. Raymond Wielgus. Ill. 10*

9 *Male figure (mimia). Wood, traces red paint, 12⅝" high. Collection Mr. and Mrs. Raymond Wielgus. Ill. 74*

10 *Female figure. Between Fly and Bamu Rivers. Coll. A. B. Lewis, 1912. Wood, traces red and black paint, 43⅝" high. Chicago 142781. Ill. 71*

11 *Female figure. Between Fly and Bamu Rivers. Wood, 40⅞" high. Coll. A. B. Lewis, 1912. Chicago 142782. Ill. 70*

12 *Male figure. Between Fly and Bamu Rivers. Coll. A. B. Lewis, 1912. Wood, 36" high. Collection Mr. and Mrs. Raymond Wielgus. Ill. 72*